Editor
Eric Migliaccio

Managing Editor
Ina Massler Levin, M.A.

Editor-in-Chief
Sharon Coan, M.S. Ed.

Illustrator
Reneé Christine Yates

Cover Artist
Denice Bauer

Art Coordinator
Kevin Barnes

Imaging
Rosa C. See

Product Manager
Phil Garcia

Publishers
Rachelle Cracchiolo, M.S. Ed.
Mary Dupuy Smith, M.S. Ed.

Nonfiction Strategies

Grades 1-3

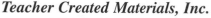

Author

Debra J. Housel, M.S. Ed.

Teacher Created Materials, Inc.
6421 Industry Way
Westminster, CA 92683
www.teachercreated.com
ISBN-0-7439-3270-6
©2002 Teacher Created Materials, Inc.
Reprinted, 2003
Made in U.S.A.

Table of Contents

Introduction

The ability to handle nonfiction information effectively has greater importance today than ever before in human history. Currently over 75 percent of all materials that are written, published, or available in on the Internet are nonfiction. In fact, so much expository text exists that we are living in an "information explosion." Your students need instruction that teaches them how to effectively read, write, discuss, research, remember, and listen to information as prerequisites for success in the 21st century. *Nonfiction Strategies* for grades 1–3 will help you to prepare them for these challenges.

Organization of this Book

Mastery of nonfiction comprehension skills comes from regular, meaningful practice over a period of time. The five steps of scaffolded instruction (Blachowicz and Ogle, 2001) provide a guide for teaching any nonfiction skill:

1. Identify and set standards-based goals.

2. Model the learning behavior.

3. Provide guided practice (lead the students through the process).

4. Provide independent practice (gradually releasing responsibility to the learners).

5. Assess student learning and performance.

Nonfiction Strategies supports all aspects of scaffolded instruction. It contains two correlation charts, nine strategy sections, and a bibliography. The strategy sections include quick and easy ideas that you can implement in 20 minutes or less, as well as strategies that encompass several lessons or an entire unit. Every strategy section includes graphic organizers; the book has a total of 42.

- The **McREL Standards Correlation Chart** identifies specific strategies to meet the standards and related benchmarks for language arts. (Copyright 2000 McREL, Mid-continent Research for Education and Learning, 2250 S. Parker Road, Suite 500, Aurora, CO 80014. Telephone: 303-337-0990.)

- A **Content Area Correlation Chart** lets you check each strategy to see if it is recommended for a specific content area.

- **Preparing Students for Nonfiction** provides ideas and strategies that will develop students' vocabulary, prior knowledge, and prediction capabilities.

- **Listening to Nonfiction** gives a variety of specific strategies proven to enhance your students' critical-listening skills and ability to glean key information and essential details from lectures, speeches, and audiovisual presentations.

- **Discussing Nonfiction** outlines ways to organize and facilitate effective and thought-provoking whole-group, small-group, and partner discussions. The discussion prompts on page 52 offer critical-thinking questions so students will grapple with issues using their higher-level thinking skills.

- **Emerging Reading and Writing Skills** gives an overview of the developmental nature of primary students' acquisition of reading and writing skills. This section lets you know what you can expect from your students.

Introduction *(cont.)*

- **Reading Nonfiction** offers techniques for helping students to comprehend what they read in expository texts.

- **Writing Nonfiction** recommends ways to develop your students' ability to write both formal and informal expository pieces.

- **Researching Nonfiction** provides a systematic approach that scaffolds your students' abilities to conduct research and prepare accurate, engaging presentations and written reports.

- **Remembering Nonfiction** suggests different research-based techniques to help move information from students' short-term memories into permanent memory storage.

- **Assessing Students' Nonfiction Comprehension** presents a wealth of ideas for authentically evaluating students' nonfiction understanding. These strategies take you beyond the confines of traditional paper-and-pencil objective tests by explaining how to create and use a portfolio system and providing five assessment tools.

- **Resources** list all the journal articles and books cited. These provide primary source information for many of the strategies.

How to Use this Book

First skim *Nonfiction Strategies* to familiarize yourself with its contents. Then choose a way to use the book most effectively. Here are some possibilities:

1. Decide which skill(s) your students will need to master the particular subject. You may choose one strategy from Preparing Students for Nonfiction, another from Reading Nonfiction, and a third from Discussing Nonfiction for the same topic or unit. Check the Content Area Correlations Chart on pages 10–15 to determine whether the strategies you've selected are recommended for the subject area. Then refer to the McRel Standards Correlation Chart on pages 5–9 to determine the standard(s) and benchmark(s) your lessons will cover.

2. Determine the McRel standard(s) and benchmark(s) you want to cover in your lesson or unit. Use the McRel Standards Correlation Chart on pages 5–9 to locate strategies that utilize those skills. Read the strategies over and pick one or more. Refer to the Content Area Correlations Chart on pages 10–15 to determine whether the strategies you have selected are recommended for the subject area.

3. If you want to use a specific strategy, refer to the Content Area Correlations Chart to determine whether those you have selected are recommended for the subject area. Then cross reference the strategy in the McRel Standards Correlation Chart to determine the standard(s) and benchmark(s) your lessons will cover.

McREL Standards Correlation

McREL Standards are in bold print.* Benchmarks are in regular print.

Standards & Benchmarks	Strategy Name	Page(s)
Language Arts (Writing)		
Demonstrates competence in the general skills and strategies of the writing process.	See Writing Nonfiction section See Emerging Reading and Writing Skills section Written retelling scoring guide	90–119 57–62 168
Uses prewriting strategies to plan written work	• Helping reluctant writers • Five-sentence paragraph • Key ideas	91 98 103
Uses strategies to edit and publish written work	• Creating nonfiction books • Nonfiction book report poster • Class alphabet book • Self-editing • Editing conferences	93 94 154 116 116
Evaluates own and others' writing	• Self-editing • Peer editing • Praise-question-polish • Nonfiction book report poster • Student's self-evaluation	116 116 118 94 174
Dictates or writes with a logical sequence of events	• Teaching sequence • Stairstep organizer • Writing about cause-effect relationships • Step-by-step graphic organizer	79 80 106 146
Dictates or writes detailed descriptions of familiar persons, places, objects, or experiences	• Learning logs • Experience writing • Writing about a past event • Writing about personal events • Writing about family members	90 93 93 92 94
Writes in response to literature	• Reaction guide • Text response centers • Creative nonfiction writing: RAFT • Internalized response	34 140 101 141
Writes in a variety of formats	• Pattern writing • Triangle poetry • Creative nonfiction writing: RAFT	92 96 101
Writes stories or essays that convey an intended purpose	• Learning to summarize: Today's story • Monthly recap	102 104
Writes expository compositions	• Pattern report • Sum-it-up chart • Creating nonfiction books • Experience writing	137 132 93 93
Writes autobiographical compositions	• Preparing an autobiography • Preparing a biography • Biopoems	110 112 114

McREL Standards Correlation *(cont.)*

Standards & Benchmarks	Strategy Name	Page(s)
Demonstrates competence in the stylistic and rhetorical aspects of writing		
Uses general, frequently used words to convey basic ideas	• Word walls • Free association • Concept building with word association	57 18 17
Uses descriptive language that clarifies and enhances ideas	• Expanding word choices • Life experiences vocabulary • Experience writing • Writing about a past event • Writing about personal events • Writing about family members	58 141 93 93 92 94
Uses paragraph form in writing	• Paragraph frame • Polar opposites • Five-sentence paragraph • Magnet summaries • Summary frame	100 100 98 108 114
Uses a variety of sentence structures	• Sentence frames • Sentence building game	61 61
Uses grammatical and mechanical conventions in written compositions.		
Uses complete sentences	• Developmental stages of spelling and writing • Developmental stages of written reports	60 57
Uses declarative and interrogative sentences in written compositions	• Sentence frames • Sentence building game • Learning logs • Internalized response	61 61 90 141
Uses nouns in written compositions	• Using nouns and active verbs • Expanding word choices	91 58
Uses verbs in written compositions	• Using nouns and active verbs • Expanding word choices	91 58
Gathers and uses information for research purposes.	See Researching Nonfiction section Research and written report scoring guide Research and presentation scoring guide	120–138 170 171
Uses a variety of strategies to identify topics to investigate	• Inquiry-based research • Selection of topic	120 121
Generates questions about topics of personal interest	• Helping students establish inquiry questions	121
Uses books to gather information for research topics	• Conducting research • Knowing where to find answers • Citing sources	123 127 138
Uses encyclopedias to gather information for research topics	• Using the library for research • Using a computer for research	127 128
Uses multiple representations of information (maps, charts, photos) to find information	• Concept organization chart • Hierarchy array	28 21

McREL Standards Correlation *(cont.)*

Standards & Benchmarks	Strategy Name	Page(s)
Uses graphic organizers to gather and record information for research topics	• Recording information • K-W-L chart • Sum-it-up chart • Query chart • Key ideas • Mind maps • Web notes	128 130 132 134 103 142 136
Compiles information into written summaries	• Bare bones summary • Cycle organizer • Magnet summaries • Sum-it-up chart • Home-school folder • Venn diagram • Stairstep sequencer	150 144 108 132 148 48 80
Language Arts (Reading)		
Demonstrates competence in the skills and strategies of the reading process	See Reading Nonfiction section See Emerging Reading & Writing Skills section Written retelling scoring guide	63–89 57–62 168
Creates mental images from pictures and print	• Envisioning text while reading • Visualizing while listening • Listening center • Word pictures • Reading aloud • Reaction guide	70 30 29 32 29 34
Uses pictures and captions to aid comprehension and to make predictions about content	• Concept attainment • Sensory vocabulary • Facial expressions • Strategic questioning	16 19 19 64
Decodes unknown words using basic elements of phonetic analysis and structural analysis	• Decoding with confidence • Phonemic awareness games • Unlocking the meanings of new words • Important word parts in English • Introducing new vocabulary	58 58 59 59 16
Reads aloud familiar stories, poems, and passages	• Readers' theater • Historical fiction builds background	34 13
Previews text	• Directed reading/thinking activity • Turning headings into questions • Strategic questioning	63 65 64
Establishes a purpose for reading	• Semantic matrix • Folded-paper questions and answers • Anticipation guide • Turning headings into questions • Thinking guide • Directed reading/thinking activity	46 66 24 65 26 63

McREL Standards Correlation *(cont.)*

Standards & Benchmarks	Strategy Name	Page(s)
Makes, confirms, and revises simple predictions about what will be found in a text	• Directed listening/thinking activity • Directed reading/thinking activity • Anticipation guide • Thinking guide	35 63 24
Monitors own reading strategies and makes modifications as needed	• Self-monitoring reading strategy • Independent reading bookmark	88 89
Identifies the author's purpose	• Questioning the author • Thinking guide	51 26
Demonstrates competence in the general skills and strategies for reading a variety of informational texts.		
Applies reading skills and strategies to a variety of informational books	• Question and answer relationships • Free association • Schema activation plan	68 18 14
Understands the main idea of simple expository information	• Identifying the main idea and supporting details • GIST: Finding the main idea • Main idea: Balancing bar • Main idea: Equation • Main idea: Horse organizer • Main idea: Main street organizer • Main idea: Umbrella organizer	72 71 38 160 74 72 40
Summarizes information found in texts in his or her own words	• 3-2-1 summary • Acrostic grid • Herringbone • Essential questions • Handy 5Ws • Informal notes outline	102 164 162 86 84 152
Relates new information to prior knowledge and experience	• Life experiences vocabulary • Before and after drawings • Quick draws • Comparison chart • List-group-label • Categorizing	141 166 20 82 45 19
Knows the defining characteristics of a variety of informational texts	• Distinguishing between fiction and nonfiction • Signal words • Text structure	13 77 76
Uses text organizers (headings, italics, graphics, etc.) to determine the main ideas and to locate information in a text	• Turning headings into questions • Strategic questioning • Knowing where to find answers	65 64 127
Identifies and uses the various parts of a book to locate information	• Distinguishing between fiction and nonfiction • Knowing where to find answers	13 127
Identifies the author's viewpoints in an informational text	• Listening to different points of view • Voice • Thinking guide	35 35 26

McREL Standards Correlation *(cont.)*

Standards & Benchmarks	Strategy Name	Page(s)
Seeks peer help to understand information	• Free association • Self-monitoring reading strategy	18 88
Language Arts (Listening and Speaking)		
Demonstrates competence in speaking and listening as tools for learning	See Listening to Nonfiction section See Discussing Nonfiction section Discussion scoring guide	29–43 44–56 169
Makes contributions in class and group discussions	• Cooperative listening • Collaborative listening/viewing guide • Brainstorming carousel • Roundtable discussions • ReQuest	37 43 56 56 65
Asks and responds to questions	• A community of learners • Asking questions before, during, and after reading • Why? Pie • Question exchange • Query chart	126 64 54 53 134
Follows the rules of conversation (taking turns, staying on topic, raising hand to speak, etc.)	• Discussion prompts • Readers guild • Class observer	52 56 44
Listens and responds to oral directions	• Listen-read-discuss • Possible sentences • Identifying facts while listening • Listening guide	36 37 36 42
Listens to and recites familiar stories, poems, and rhymes with patterns	• Songs and rhymes • Listening to stories	139 32
Listens and responds to a variety of media	• Readers' theater • Film discussion • A picture is worth a thousand words • Television show summary • Collaborative listening/viewing guide	34 42 21 102 43
Listens to classmates and adults	• Taking a stand • Surveys • ReQuest • Guided discovery	50 124 65 17
Makes some effort to have a clear main point when speaking to others	• Discussion prompts • Discussing emotions • Text response centers • Taking a stand	52 50 140 50
Organizes ideas for oral presentations	• Jackdaws • Guided imagery	138 137

*Kendall, John S., Marzano, Robert J. (1997) *Content Knowledge: A Compendium of Standards and Benchmarks for K–12 Education, 2nd Ed.* Aurora, CO. McREL. Used by permission of McREL.

Content Area Correlation Chart

This alphabetical list shows you in which content area(s) each strategy works well.

Strategy Name	Page	Social Studies	Science	Math
3-2-1 summary	102	✓	✓	✓
A picture is worth a thousand words	21	✓	✓	
Acronyms	139	✓	✓	
Acrostic grid	164	✓	✓	✓
Anticipation guide	24	✓	✓	✓
Asking questions before, during, and after reading	64	✓	✓	✓
Bare bones summary	150	✓	✓	
Before and after drawings	166	✓	✓	
Biopoems	114	✓		
Brainstorming carousel	56	✓		
Categorizing	19	✓	✓	✓
Citing sources	138	✓	✓	
Class alphabet book	154	✓	✓	✓
Class observer	44	✓	✓	
Collaborative listening/viewing guide	43	✓	✓	✓
Community of learners	126	✓	✓	
Comparison chart	82	✓		
Concept attainment	16	✓	✓	✓
Concept building with word association	17	✓	✓	
Concept organization chart	28	✓	✓	
Cooperative listening	37	✓	✓	✓
Creating nonfiction books	93	✓	✓	
Creative nonfiction writing: RAFT	101	✓	✓	✓
Cycle organizer	144	✓	✓	
Directed listening/thinking activity	35	✓	✓	✓
Directed reading/thinking activity	63	✓	✓	✓
Discussing emotions	50	✓	✓	
Discussion prompts	52	✓	✓	
Distinguishing between fiction and nonfiction	13	✓	✓	
Editing conferences	116	✓	✓	
Educator observation checklists	157	✓	✓	
Envisioning text while reading	70	✓	✓	
Essential questions	86	✓		
Expanding word choices	58	✓	✓	
Experience writing	93	✓		
Facial expressions	19	✓		
Film discussion	42	✓		
Five fingers	139	✓	✓	✓
Five-sentence paragraph	98	✓	✓	
Folded-paper questions and answers	66	✓	✓	
Free association	18	✓	✓	
GIST: Finding the main idea	71	✓	✓	
Guided discovery	17	✓	✓	✓
Guided imagery	137	✓	✓	
Handy 5Ws	84	✓	✓	
Helping reluctant writers	91	✓	✓	
Herringbone	162	✓		

Content Area Correlation Chart

Strategy Name	Page	Social Studies	Science	Math
Hierarchy array	21	✓	✓	
Historical fiction builds background knowledge	13	✓		
Home-school folder	148	✓	✓	✓
Identifying elements of a set	159		✓	✓
Identifying facts while listening	36	✓	✓	✓
Identifying main idea and supporting details	72	✓	✓	
Important word parts in English	59	✓	✓	
Independent reading bookmark	89	✓	✓	✓
Informal notes outline	152	✓	✓	
Inquiry-based research	120	✓	✓	
Internalized response	141	✓	✓	
Introducing new vocabulary	16	✓	✓	
Jackdaws	138	✓	✓	
Knowing where to find answers	127	✓	✓	✓
Knowledge rating	22	✓	✓	✓
K-W-L chart	130	✓	✓	✓
Learning logs	90	✓	✓	✓
Learning to summarize: Today's story	102	✓		
Life experiences vocabulary	141	✓		
Listening center	29	✓	✓	
Listening for context	37	✓	✓	
Listening guide	42	✓	✓	✓
Listening to different points of view	35	✓		
Listening to stories	32	✓		
Listen-read-discuss	36	✓	✓	✓
List-group-label	45	✓	✓	
Magnet summaries	108	✓	✓	✓
Main idea: Balancing bar	38	✓	✓	
Main idea: Equation organizer	160	✓	✓	✓
Main idea: Horse organizer	74	✓	✓	
Main idea: Main Street organizer	72	✓	✓	
Main idea: Umbrella organizer	40	✓	✓	
Maze	159	✓	✓	
Mind maps	142	✓	✓	✓
Monthly recap	103	✓	✓	✓
Nonfiction book report poster	94	✓	✓	
Paragraph frame	100	✓	✓	✓
Pattern report	137	✓	✓	
Pattern writing	92	✓	✓	✓
Peer editing	116	✓	✓	
Performances	156	✓	✓	✓
Polar opposites	100	✓	✓	✓
Portfolios	156	✓	✓	✓
Possible sentences	37	✓	✓	
Praise-question-polish	118	✓	✓	
Preparing a biography	112	✓		
Preparing an autobiography	110	✓		
Query chart	134	✓	✓	
Question exchange	53	✓	✓	✓
Question-answer relationships	68	✓	✓	

Content Area Correlation Chart

Strategy Name	Page	Social Studies	Science	Math
Questioning the author	51	✓	✓	
Quick draws	20	✓	✓	✓
Reaction guide	34	✓	✓	
Readers' guild	56	✓		
Readers' theater	34	✓	✓	
Reading aloud	29	✓	✓	
Recording information	128	✓	✓	✓
ReQuest	65	✓	✓	
Roundtable discussion	56	✓		
Schema activation plan	14	✓	✓	
Self-editing	116	✓	✓	
Self-monitoring reading strategy	88	✓	✓	✓
Semantic matrix	46	✓	✓	
Sensory vocabulary	19	✓	✓	
Sentence building game	61	✓	✓	
Sentence frames	61	✓	✓	✓
Signal words	77	✓	✓	
Songs and rhymes	139	✓	✓	✓
Stairstep sequencer	80	✓		
Step-by-step graphic organizer	146	✓	✓	✓
Strategic questioning	64	✓	✓	
Student self-evaluation	157	✓	✓	✓
Sum-it-up chart	132	✓		
Summary frame	114	✓	✓	✓
Surveys	124	✓	✓	✓
Taking a stand	50	✓	✓	
Teaching cause and effect	77	✓	✓	✓
Teaching comparisons	82	✓	✓	✓
Teaching inferential skills	76	✓	✓	
Teaching sequence	79	✓	✓	✓
Television show summary	102	✓	✓	
Text response centers	140	✓	✓	
Text structure	76	✓	✓	
Thinking guide	26	✓	✓	
Triangle poetry graphic organizer	96	✓	✓	
Turning headings into questions	65	✓	✓	✓
Unlocking the meanings of new words	59	✓	✓	
Using a computer for research	128	✓	✓	
Using nouns and active verbs	91	✓	✓	
Using the library for research	127	✓	✓	
Venn diagram	48	✓	✓	
Visualizing while listening	30	✓	✓	
Voice	35	✓	✓	
Web notes	136	✓	✓	
Why? Pie	54	✓	✓	
Word pictures	32	✓		
Word walls	57	✓	✓	✓
Writing about a past event	94	✓		
Writing about family members	93	✓		
Writing about cause-effect relationships	106	✓	✓	✓
Writing about personal events	92	✓		

Introduction to Section 1: Preparing Students for Nonfiction

Teaching nonfiction means "arousing the curiosity of students, assessing their present understandings, exploring with them some of the possibilities for study about the topic, and . . . setting the stage for learning to take place" (Parker, 2001). This section offers you techniques for getting students to think about what they already know about a topic so that they can take in new information and add it to their store of knowledge in the most effective way. Research has repeatedly proven that the larger a person's store of information, the more apt he or she is to successfully comprehend and learn any new material encountered in nonfiction.

Competent readers and listeners always make connections. They interact with information, consciously thinking of questions, revising predictions, and eliminating misconceptions. For information to enter long-term memory, students must integrate new data with their previous store of knowledge. They also need to be able to use this new knowledge by transferring it to different or new situations. In addition, authors expect readers to use their own experiences and knowledge to interact with information. This means that your students must learn the inferential skills necessary to "read between the lines" and understand implied ideas that are not stated. For methods of developing students' inferential skills, see Reading Nonfiction.

Nonfiction text is packed with both concepts and vocabulary. Therefore, before students can effectively comprehend nonfiction material, you must always build their background knowledge (schema). If your students are unfamiliar with a topic you are about to study, it is crucial for you to spend time building their knowledge foundation with the activities presented in this section.

Strategies: Fiction and Nonfiction; Background Knowledge

❖ Distinguishing Between Fiction and Nonfiction

Help your students to understand how nonfiction differs from fiction by reading aloud a short story (example, an Aesop's fable) and a short nonfiction article (example, *Time for Kids* magazine). Then guide a class discussion with these questions:

- How are nonfiction articles and fictional stories the same?
- How are nonfiction articles and fictional stories different?
- Why are fictional stories and nonfiction articles different?
- Should we read nonfiction articles the same way that we read fictional stories? Explain.

❖ Historical Fiction Builds Background Knowledge

Read aloud historical fiction with child protagonists to build background knowledge and interest. For example, reading *The Courage of Sarah Noble* prior to studying the Eastern Woodland Native American culture will help students to genuinely want to know more about this group of people. Laura Ingalls Wilder's *Farmer Boy* and *Little House* books have sparked generations of children's enthusiasm about the American way of life during the 19th century.

Strategies: Schema Activation

❖ Schema Activation Plan

Try using a schema activation plan (Frayer, et al., 1969) prior to reading a nonfiction passage.

Preview the material; select a key concept; and then choose a phrase, picture, or word to represent it to your class to initiate a discussion.

Ask students to brainstorm everything they know about the topic. Brainstorming is very important, since listening to the associations and explanations of others causes students to add to their own knowledge and helps you to determine the level of prior knowledge that your students have about the subject. It encourages academically weak students by letting them know that they already have some knowledge about the topic.

Create a master list of student ideas.

Help the students to summarize what they've learned through the use of the graphic organizer on page 15. Here is an example:

What are mammals?	
What are the most important features? • breathe air • have hair or fur • warm blooded	***What are other features?*** • babies are born alive • babies look like their parents • some hibernate in the winter
What are some examples? tiger whale bat beaver cat dog people cow sea otter	***What are not examples?*** frog fish bug snake spider robin

Strategies: Schema Activation Plan *(cont.)*

Graphic Organizer

What are _____ ?

What are the most important features?	**What are other features?**
What are some examples?	**What are *not* examples?**

Strategies: Concept Attainment; New Vocabulary

✛ Concept Attainment

Closely related to a schema activation plan is concept attainment (Joyce and Weil, 1999). Both require students to use higher level thinking skills by gathering information, comparing and contrasting examples, establishing generalizations, and applying the concept to new situations.

1. Tell students the concept's label, as well as the essential attributes of the concept.

2. Provide examples of the concept (preferably visuals).

3. Provide non-examples of the concept (especially those that the students may misidentify as examples of the concept).

4. Present both examples and non-examples and ask students to distinguish between them.

5. Have students find or draw examples and non-examples on their own (by looking through old magazines, cutting out pictures, and taping them on a sheet of butcher paper divided into two labeled sections, such as "Examples of Reptiles" and "Non-examples of Reptiles")

✛ Introducing New Vocabulary

Select a main concept that the students need to know. Display the word. Give the students three minutes in which to tell you as many related terms as possible. Record a master list of student ideas underneath the concept word. Then add new vocabulary terms and discuss them. Suppose you are going to read about how caverns are formed. You select the basic concept of caves and list the students' ideas:

cold	dark	animal home	scary
rocks	water	cavemen	blind fish
animal home	underground	coal mine	in hillside
labyrinth	*stalagmite*	*stalactite*	*spelunker*

After the students have stated everything they already know, add the concepts (italicized) you want to introduce. Since the students have established a frame of reference, their minds will more readily incorporate these new concepts. You can also draw an analogy between coal mines (manmade tunnels) and caverns (naturally formed passageways).

Strategies: Concept Building; Guided Discovery

✤ Concept Building with Word Association

Bolster your students' vocabulary by displaying words from an upcoming topic. As students come up with words that relate to each, write their responses. In this example, the teacher displayed the boldface words and the students supplied the ones beneath:

<table>
<tr><td colspan="2">transport</td><td colspan="2">expressway</td></tr>
<tr><td>move</td><td>carry</td><td>traffic</td><td>vehicles</td></tr>
<tr><td>airplane</td><td>truck</td><td>highway</td><td>road</td></tr>
<tr><td>train</td><td>cars</td><td>exit</td><td>signs</td></tr>
</table>

Another word association strategy makes good educational use of a few minutes' unscheduled time. Display some words related to a topic that the class has been studying (for example, *castle, turret, moat, drawbridge,* and *knight*). Then state a word and ask for volunteers to choose a word on the board that relates to it and explain how it relates. Following the same example, you could say these words: a ditch? a palace? a student? an ocean? a soldier? a tower? a mansion? a guard? You may be surprised by what the students will find a relationship for and the good reasons they will give!

✤ Guided Discovery

Guided discovery teaches children new vocabulary by utilizing their own life experiences to figure out the meaning of unknown words in context. Pull out the vocabulary-containing sentences from a nonfiction passage and present them. Through questions and discussion, guide the students to discover the meanings. This helps children to determine the meaning of unknown words through the use of context coupled with their own background knowledge. For example, you present this statement: "Some materials, such as metal, conduct electricity better than other materials."

Teacher: What can you tell about the word *conduct* from the sentence?
Student: It has to do with electricity.
Teacher: Right. What does it mention conducts electricity well?
Student: Metals.
Teacher: Think about electricity in your own home. How do you use metal with electricity there?
Student: Well, the ends of plugs are metal.
Teacher: Yes. They're called prongs. How do you plug something in?
Student: You stick the metal prongs into a thing in the wall—into an outlet.
Teacher: And then what happens?
Student: The lamp lights up.
Teacher: Why does the lamp light?
Student: Because it's getting electricity.
Teacher: Through the metal prongs?
Student: Yes.
Teacher: So what do you think *conduct* means?
Student: Move. The metal lets the electricity move from the wall to the lamp.
Teacher: Why is it important to know this?
Student: Because it tells us how electricity moves.
Teacher: Now that we know this, is it okay to stick a metal knife in a toaster that's turned on?
Student: No!
Teacher: Why?
Student: Because the electricity could be conducted to me and it would hurt.

Strategies: Free Association

❖ Free Association

Activate background knowledge through free association by presenting students with the two major concepts of expository text and asking them to brainstorm a list of ideas related to each. Challenge them to find a way in which the items in the lists relate to each other.

Suppose you plan to read an article about the controversy over a proposed dam that is needed for flood control but that will cause important archaeological digs, ancient cemeteries, statues, and buildings to be deep under water. Divide the class in half. The students in one half of the class will have two minutes to individually brainstorm a list of words relating to dams. At the same time the students in the other half of the class will individually brainstorm a list of words relating to ancient things. (Be sure that your students know what *ancient* means.)

Dams	
big	floods
concrete	power
gates	water
lake/river	protect
necessary	beaver

Ancient Things	
pyramids	antiques
graveyards	very old
can't be replaced	long ago
valuable	in museums
dinosaurs	cavepeople

Reconvene the class and create a class list. Form student teams of three. Each team should generate pairs of words (one word from each list) that they can orally defend. The mental processing used to create these pairs will prepare students for the material. Words can be paired more than once. Here's an example:

> *big and pyramids:* "The pyramids are very big."
>
> *big and dinosaurs:* "Dinosaurs are really big, too."
>
> *protect and antiques:* "Mom protects her antiques. She won't let me touch ours."
>
> *necessary and graveyards:* "Graveyards are necessary."
>
> *floods and cavepeople:* "Cavepeople were afraid of drowning in floods."
>
> *floods and can't be replaced:* "Floods wash away things that can't be replaced."

Notice the evidence of the following:

- ✦ a rudimentary understanding of the size of a dam as related to other large things (pyramids, dinosaurs)
- ✦ the need to protect ancient things
- ✦ the fear of floods due to drowning
- ✦ the recognition that floods eliminate irreplaceable things

Strategies: Sensory Vocabulary; Facial Expressions; Categorizing

✣ Sensory Vocabulary

Prepare a list of vocabulary. Present several important words that can be visualized or that can evoke the senses. Avoid concept words like *freedom*, for which the students cannot generate visual or sensory images. For example, if you are going to read about how moss must live in a shady, damp area where it can absorb water, you might select these words: *moss*, *shade*, *damp*, and *absorb*. Have students stare at a picture of a word for 30 seconds. Then have them close their eyes and recreate that picture in their minds. Do the same for each vocabulary word that can be illustrated. Be creative. For words that cannot be illustrated—such as *damp* and *absorb*—demonstrate how a paper towel absorbs a spill and then pass around the damp paper towel.

✣ Facial Expressions

If a text says that a person was terrified, shocked, disappointed, or puzzled, and your students do not know what that facial expression looks like, they will be unable to create an accurate mental image. Search old newspapers, magazines, and books for different facial expressions. Mount them on construction paper or tagboard and discuss each one with the class. Identify what words a writer might use to describe each facial expression. Record these words on the back of each picture. Post the pictures. Then when the text says: "The people in the lifeboats watched as the *Titanic* slipped beneath the cold, dark surface of the Atlantic Ocean," you can ask your students to identify what their facial expressions may have been.

✣ Categorizing

Categorization activities help students make inferences about clusters of related nouns. In this example, the students need to put each term under the person most apt to have frequent contact with it in his or her job. Each word can be placed in only one of the columns.

axe	badge	helmet	gun	hose	needle	car
bandage	pills	handcuffs	patients	cast	truck	smoke

Firefighter	Police Officer	Doctor
axe	badge	needle
helmet	gun	bandage
hose	car	pills
truck	handcuffs	patients
smoke		cast

The chart may spark discussion about where certain words belong—such as *car*. All of the occupations may involve driving a car to work, but police officers are the ones most apt to patrol in a car. You can expand the chart throughout the unit by adding columns and characteristics of other occupations.

Strategies: Quick Draws

✛ Quick Draws

Quick draws prepare students to assimilate new material by having them mentally retrieve and draw previously learned material. Suppose that you are going to read a passage about pollution. First, make sure that students know what the word means. Then state: "In the next two minutes I want you to quickly draw a picture of pollution, including any details you can recall." A student might draw:

Obviously, this student has some prior knowledge of pollution. Starting out with a quick draw helps students to feel less overwhelmed when asked to read or listen to an article. It makes them recognize that they already know something about the subject. The realization that they possess some knowledge is exciting and empowering, especially for students who struggle.

Strategies: Pictures; Hierarchy Array

⁜ A Picture Is Worth a Thousand Words

Show a documentary or fictional film prior to teaching about a topic about which students may lack prior knowledge. For example, before studying killer whales, have your students watch a film such as *Free Willy*. (Watch the film first to be certain that the film is appropriate for your grade level. Depending on your district's policy, you may also need written parental permission before showing a fictional film.)

⁜ Hierarchy Array

A hierarchy array provides a good overview prior to studying something that has classifications and categories. The following is an example:

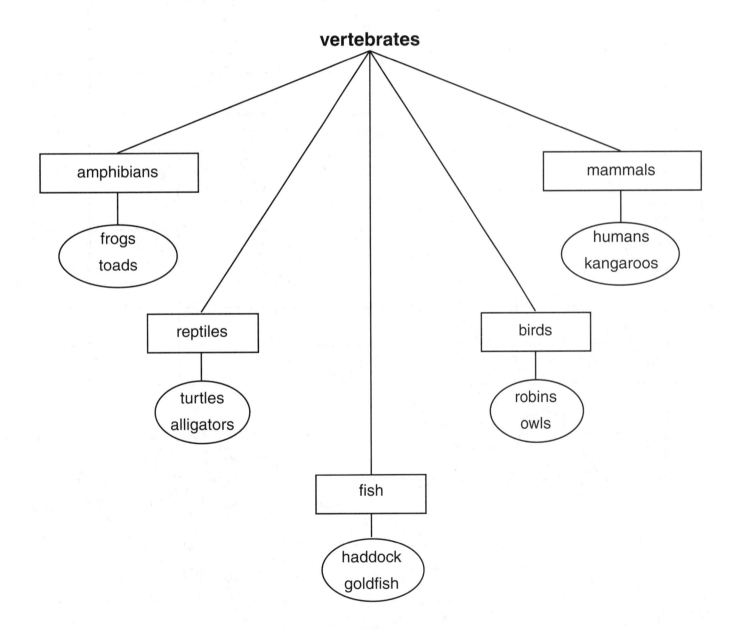

Strategies: Knowledge Rating

✛ Knowledge Rating

You can quickly discern what your students already know about the specialized vocabulary of a topic with a knowledge rating sheet (Blachowicz and Ogle, 2001). Well in advance of a unit of study, choose five vocabulary words that are crucial to understanding an upcoming expository passage. Using the blank template on page 23, prepare a knowledge rating sheet as shown in the example and make photocopies. Distribute the knowledge rating sheet to each student and read the words aloud (so that decoding is not an issue). Depending on the needs of your class, give the students between 45 seconds and one minute to fill in the sheet and submit it to you. Then you can review the sheets to see what you need to concentrate on in your upcoming lessons. Here is an example:

Knowledge Rating

Topic: Holidays			
Directions: Put a checkmark (✔) in the column that tells how well you know each of these words.			
Word	**I know what it means.**	**I have heard it before.**	**I do not know it.**
Halloween	✔		
Thanksgiving	✔		
Kwanzaa		✔	
Yom Kippur			✔
First Day of Ramadan			✔

Strategies: Knowledge Rating (cont.)

Graphic Organizer

Name _____

Knowledge Rating

Topic:			
Directions: Put a checkmark (✓) in the column that tells how well you know each of these words.			
Word	**I know what it means.**	**I have heard it before.**	**I do not know it.**

 #3270 Nonfiction Strategies—Grades 1–3

Strategies: Anticipation Guide

✢ Anticipation Guide

Use an anticipation guide to assess prior knowledge and to determine if your students have misconceptions about a topic. Using the graphic organizer on page 25, create an anticipation guide with a total of three true-or-false statements. Distribute the guide to the students and read the statements to the students (so you are checking knowledge rather than decoding ability). Then ask the students to mark each statement true or false.

After reading or listening to the information, have students fix any statements they marked incorrectly by writing a brief explanation of the correct answer. For example:

Anticipation Guide

Directions: Read the sentences. Think about what you know. Put **T** for "true" or **F** for "false."

___F___ 1. Everyone in the world lives in the same type of home.

___T___ 2. Homes give people shelter and a place to rest.

___F___ 3. More than one family can share a home.

   People from different families can live together in one house.
   Sometimes families new to our nation live together.

Strategies: Anticipation Guide *(cont.)*

Graphic Organizer

Directions: Before you read about _____ ,
look at these sentences. Based on what you already know about the topic, write **T**
on the line if the statement is true and **F** on the line if the statement is false.

_____ 1.

_____ 2.

_____ 3.

Strategies: Thinking Guide

✢ Thinking Guide

A thinking guide (Herber, 1978) not only gives your students a preview of the important concepts or issues that will be raised in an article, it causes them to compare their ideas to the author's. Fill out the thinking guide graphic organizer on page 27. Photocopy and distribute the guide. Read the statements to the students (so that you are checking knowledge rather than decoding ability). In the "Me" column, the student places an "A" for agree if he or she believes the statement or a "D" for disagree if he or she believes the statement is wrong.

After listening to or reading the article, the student fills in the Author column. At the bottom of the page the student writes a brief summary of he or she they learned from the passage. Here is an example:

Directions: Read each sentence. In the "Me" column, write an **A** if you agree or write a **D** if you do not agree. You will fill in the rest later.

	Me	Author
1. Long ago, birds and smoke were used for long distance communications.	D	A
2. The Pony Express was the first United States mail service.	A	D
3. Today, long distance communication is easier than ever before.	A	A

What did you learn?

Native Americans used smoke signals for messages. Pigeons carried notes to the front lines in a war. The Pony Express was not the first U.S. mail service. It only lasted two years. Now phones and computers make long distance communication easy.

Strategies: Thinking Guide *(cont.)*

Graphic Organizer

Directions: Read each sentence. In the **Me** column, write an **A** if you agree or write a **D** if you do not agree. You will fill in the rest later.

	Me	Author
1.	_____	_____
2.	_____	_____
3.	_____	_____

What did you learn?

Strategies: Concept Organization

✢ Concept Organization Chart

Concept organization charts ensure all students have a frame of reference. Suppose you are going to read about being a veterinarian. Select a broad category—in this instance, pets. Create a simple graphic like the one shown below by having the class decide on six typical pets and listing them on the board. Guide the students to come up with the pros and cons of owning that kind of pet and list them beneath. This activates the students' schema about the pets they own while providing valuable information to the students who have never owned that kind of pet.

Pets

dog		cat		bird		fish		rabbit		hamster	
+	−	+	−	+	−	+	−	+	−	+	−

dog
- +
  - smart
  - play ball
  - learn tricks
  - protect you
  - play
- −
  - shed
  - vet bills
  - need grooming
  - need a lot of attention

cat
- +
  - pretty
  - soft
  - purr
  - play
- −
  - shed
  - scratch
  - litterbox
  - vet bills
  - trigger allergies

bird
- +
  - pretty
  - sing
  - easy to take care of
- −
  - messy
  - don't play

fish
- +
  - easy to take care of
  - not very expensive
- −
  - dull
  - can't play
  - die easily

rabbit
- +
  - soft
  - cuddly
  - pretty
- −
  - cage needs frequent cleaning

hamster
- +
  - cute
  - soft
  - fun to watch
- −
  - bite
  - get lost easily
  - don't live long

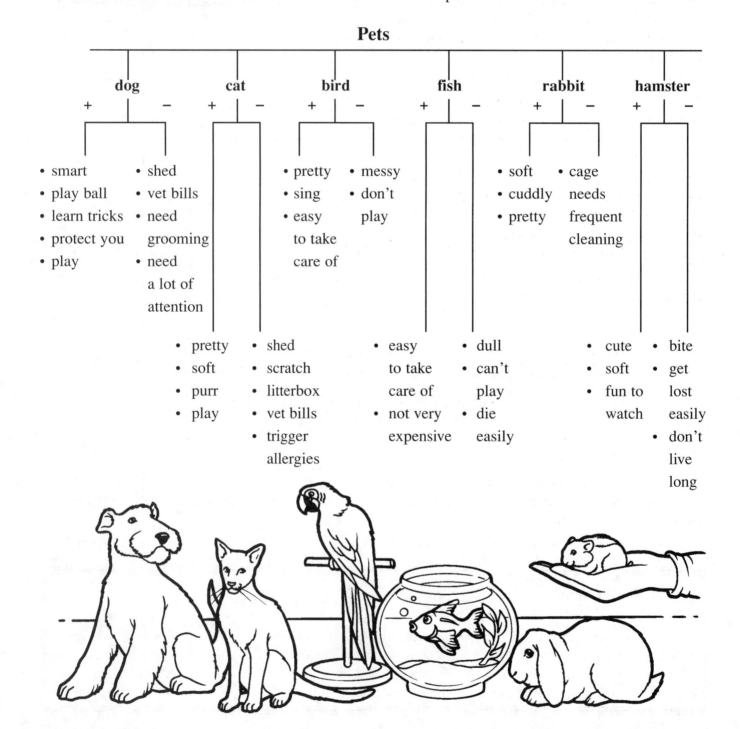

28

Introduction to Section 2: Listening to Nonfiction

The academic environment demands that students have good listening skills because listening permeates every facet of school curriculum. Research has also proven that acquiring better listening skills yields substantial benefits in reading comprehension. Consequently, we all want our students to become better listeners, to understand and remember the information they hear.

Since the ability to take notes while listening is necessary for success in high school and college, the development of these skills should begin early in a student's educational career. Taking notes promotes active listening, and educational studies have shown that the cognitive processes associated with hearing, comprehending, and writing provide the best reinforcement of material. The strategies in this section develop your students' note-taking skills using a variety of methods, including informal outlines, semantic mapping, and graphic organizers.

A person's listening level is the level at which he or she can comprehend material read or spoken aloud. Research has established that a person's listening level is approximately two years above his or her reading level. It is crucial that students of all ages hear informational text read aloud in order to increase their knowledge of language structure and vocabulary, improve writing skills, introduce new genres, and strengthen comprehension.

While careful listening is an important goal, use closed captioning as an added support during videos, films, etc. This helps novice readers match written words to spoken words. It benefits students with minor hearing impairments and speakers of English as a second language, as well as provides support to those who feel overwhelmed by information presented aurally.

Like reading, listening is a receptive skill that relies upon visualization skills. Listening comprehension can best be described as seeing a movie in the mind. Listening comprehension cannot exist without visualization.

Strategies: Listening Center; Reading Aloud

✤ Listening Center

Set up a listening center filled with short, illustrated nonfiction books on tape. Have the students listen to the entire tape without any access to the book. Then have them read the book, either with the tape's support or independently.

Ask, "How do the pictures compare to the ones that you saw in your mind? Do the illustrations help you to understand the material better?" You can also ask them to write two or three sentences comparing the book's illustrations to the pictures they formed in their minds.

✤ Reading Aloud

Of course, one of the best ways to prepare students to read expository text is to a read aloud a brief nonfiction selection every day. Reading expository text aloud is critical to developing children's ability to read it. Your students need to hear the vocabulary and complex sentence structures of written language. In addition, reading aloud a nonfiction alphabet book provides an excellent overview of a topic.

Strategies: Visualizing

✤ Visualizing While Listening

When you introduce this essential skill, start with fiction because students have had the most experience with this form. Ask your students to close their eyes and keep them closed throughout the exercise. If students find that impossible, offer blindfolds. Start out reading one or two sentences at a time, stopping frequently to guide the visualization process. Hesitate after each statement or question you make during the visualization. Emphasize that the students should answer the questions in their minds, not aloud. In this transcript, the italicized words are the text, and the quotes are the teacher's visualization guidance:

> *Once upon a time long, long ago, there was a cottage in a clearing of a deep, dark, forest.*
>
> "Picture the cottage in your mind. What is it made of—bricks, cobblestones, wood? What's the roof made of? Is the cottage pretty or old and falling down? Does it have windows? How many?"
>
> *Inside the cottage lived a family of trolls.*
>
> "Look at the trolls. What do they look like? How tall are they? Do they have hair? What color is it? What color eyes do they have? What color skin? Are all the trolls the same size? Do they look alike? How many trolls are in the family? Does knowing that trolls live inside change your image of the cottage?"

After the class has heard the story in this manner, give each student the opportunity to respond to at least one question that was not answered in the text, such as the following:

- ✦ How big is the clearing?
- ✦ What kinds of trees are in the deep, dark forest?
- ✦ What is nearby the cottage?
- ✦ What does the inside of the cottage look like?

Your students may protest, "But the author didn't tell us that." Explain that what's important is what they imagined when they heard it. People who actively visualize while listening and reading are often disappointed by a movie adapted from a book because their own images are more meaningful to them than the movie producer's version.

Next, read aloud a simple nonfiction text about a familiar animal and encourage students to incorporate their prior knowledge as they keep their eyes closed and imagine the scene. When you've finished, discuss what they saw in their minds. For example, after you read this sentence, "Woodchucks live in burrows in fields," stop and tell the students to see the field in their minds. Then ask questions that can only be answered through visualization, such as the following:

- ✦ What is growing in the field? Is there tall grass? Trees? What kinds?
- ✦ Farm crops? What kinds? Flowers? What kinds? Weeds? What kinds?
- ✦ What season is it?
- ✦ What sounds do you hear in the field?
- ✦ Can you smell anything?
- ✦ What is nearby?
- ✦ Is this a field that you've actually seen somewhere? Where?

Praise those students who add details from their visualizations. Stress that good listeners form "movies in their minds" from both the information they hear coupled with their own background knowledge.

Strategies: Visualizing *(cont.)*

Finally, walk your students through a nonfiction piece, asking them to imagine the scene using all of their senses (Rose, 1991). For example, if you are going to read about the Paul Revere's midnight ride, have the students close their eyes as you read.

The following transcript shows the text in italics and what the teacher said in quotation marks:

Paul Revere watched the bell tower of the old stone church. He waited for the light to tell him if the British were coming by land or by sea.

"Think of old stone churches you may have seen. What does the old stone church's bell tower look like? Think of old train lanterns or camping lanterns you may have seen. What will the lantern signal he's waiting for look like? It's an April evening. Is the moon out? Are there stars in the sky or is it cloudy?"

Suddenly, two flickering lights appeared in the church bell tower. The British were coming by sea to get the guns that the colonists stored in Concord!

"See the lantern flash twice. How does Paul Revere feel? What is he thinking? What will he do next?"

"Picture Paul Revere racing through the streets of town on his horse. What is Paul wearing? What is the expression on his face? What is he thinking? What is he feeling? Is the night air cold? What does his horse look like? Hear the horse's hooves as they clatter over the cobblestone streets."

Continue to work your way through the text in this manner. Then put the students into groups of three. Ask them to collaboratively draw three images showing how they envisioned the beginning, middle, and end. The group members should first discuss and decide what three images they will draw. Next, they should divide the work, with each student doing one of the drawings. Finally, they should label each other's illustrations with a sentence or caption.

Strategies: Word Pictures; Listening to Stories

✛ Word Pictures

Select a nonfiction piece that creates vivid mental images. Read the children a short passage without showing the illustrations. Then record on chart paper their responses to this question: Which word(s) painted a picture in your mind?

✛ Listening to Stories

Invite a storyteller to tell a folk tale to your class. African- and Native-American folk tales are especially good. Afterwards, have your students draw a detailed color picture of the most important or interesting mental image they envisioned while listening. Give them at least 10 minutes. Have them evaluate their images using the graphic organizer on page 33. Here's an example based on the African folk tale, "Mufaro's Beautiful Daughters":

	Yes	No
1. Does my picture have details? List them: Nyasha and the snake in her garden.	✓	
2. Did I add my own idea(s) to what I heard? Tell more: vegetables and flowers the sun in the sky Manyara hiding behind a bush		✓
3. Does my picture show feelings? Which one(s)? Tell more: Nyasha is happy and singing. The snake is smiling. Manyara is frowning. She is jealous.	✓	
4. Which senses did I use to make this image? Circle them: (see) (hear) smell taste (touch)	✓	

Put a checkmark (✓) next to what I did best.

Strategies: Listening to Stories *(cont.)*

Graphic Organizer

	Yes	No
1. Does my picture have details? List them:		
2. Did I add my own idea(s) to what I heard? Tell more:		
3. Does my picture show feelings? Which one(s)? Tell more:		
4. Which senses did I use to make this image? Circle them: **see hear smell taste touch**		

Put a checkmark (✔) next to what I did best.

Strategies: Reaction Guide; Readers' Theater

⊹ Reaction Guide

Explain to your students that authors use words to create visual images and emotional reactions in the reader. A Reaction Guide (Wood, et al., 1992) allows students to react as they listen. This makes the listening task more interactive, resulting in greater comprehension of what's been heard.

Have your students draw a vertical line in their learning logs, leaving more room on the right hand side than on the left. As the students listen to an expository text, have them record striking words, images, or phrases that evoke a response (positive or negative) in them in the left-hand column. When they have finished listening, ask them to write an explanation for why the words, images, or phrases caused them to react in the right hand column. Model this activity several times before asking the students to do it independently. For example:

Ideas, words, or phrases that caused a reaction	Because
Indians	I am part Native American. I do not like to be called an Indian. We were the first Americans!
cornbread	I like eating cornbread.
venison	I have never tried venison.
wooden huts	The Iroquois lived in longhouses. A hut sounds like something thrown together quickly.

⊹ Readers' Theater

Hearing material read aloud by readers with expressive voices brings expository text to life. Round-robin read alouds cannot accomplish this. Readers' Theater works because it provides students with the opportunity to practice the material they will read aloud, allowing even your most challenged students to read with expression, fluency, and confidence.

Assign each student one page of a short nonfiction book written at the students' independent reading level. Attach a note requesting parental assistance by having each student practice reading his or her page to the parent the night before they do so in class. The student should read it multiple times to gain fluency.

If a nonfiction text lends itself to only four student readers, select a heterogeneous group of students (one advanced student, two average students, and one struggling student) to meet and practice. Then they take turns reading aloud while the rest of the class listens. Due to the prior rehearsal component, your struggling readers will have a chance to shine with the advanced and average children—a thrilling accomplishment for those challenged by reading.

Sometimes, you may want to completely rewrite the text by having the facts spoken by a variety of characters. Assign students to these roles and give them time to practice.

Strategies: Listening/Thinking; Voice; Points of View

⁜ Directed Listening/Thinking Activity

Predictions encourage students to use prior knowledge and set a purpose for reading. The Directed Listening/Thinking Activity (Stauffer, 1969) improves young students' ability to make predictions. Start by reading the text in advance to determine good stopping points. Show the students the book's cover or illustrations and ask them to predict what the passage might be about. Ask the students to commit to one of the predictions. Next, read aloud to the first predetermined stopping point. Make a prediction—"I'd guess that . . . will happen next." Ask if the students agree with your prediction. If they don't, have them state their own. Remember to occasionally give a wrong prediction: if yours are always right, the students will stop suggesting their own.

Read aloud to the next stopping point. Ask for more student predictions. Continue in this manner until you reach the end of the passage. Discuss the predictions made and how things would have changed if the incorrect predictions had occurred.

⁜ Voice

To introduce how voice affects a composition, read aloud several short nonfiction selections, some written in first person and others written in third person. Ask the students: From whose viewpoint are we hearing this? How do you know? Brainstorm a list of advantages and disadvantages for writing in both the first- and third-person.

⁜ Listening to Different Points of View

Help students to learn that articles are written from different points of view and for different purposes. Just think of how—depending upon who the writer is—the points of view would differ on Christopher Columbus, Malcolm X, and Betty Friedman. Highlight the concept of point of view by reading aloud any version of the classic *The Three Little Pigs*, followed by Jon Scieszka's *The True Story of the Three Little Pigs* (Viking, 1999). Follow these readings with these critical thinking questions:

◆ How would it have changed the piece if the writer had used the other voice?

◆ Why do you think the two versions of the same story were so different?

◆ What effect did having a different narrator have on the stories?

Strategies: Identifying Facts; Listen-Read-Discuss

✛ Identifying Facts While Listening

Students must listen critically to assess the relevance of information. A good initial activity to help students sort out fact from fiction is to read aloud Lynne Cherry's *The Great Kapok Tree* (Voyager Picture Book, 2000). This book features talking animals who give facts about the rain forest. Make sure that your students realize that the animals' speech is fiction but that the information they are saying is not. The students may also notice that the animals are giving the facts from the point of view that the rain forest is their home and, therefore, have a vested interest in ending its destruction.

Students must listen critically to assess the truth of information. Be sure that they understand that facts are as follows:

- ◆ a number of things observed

- ◆ actions that can be observed

- ◆ physical features of thing or person

- ◆ words specifically written or said by someone (it's a fact that they said or wrote that information). Of course, what was said or written may be an opinion.

Read aloud a sentence from a nonfiction book. Have students raise their hands if they believe the statement is a fact. Work through the passage in this manner, sentence-by-sentence. Review the correct answers and add any that the students missed. After you've done this with the whole class, have the students work in pairs to read a simple photocopied passage and highlight only the facts.

✛ Listen-Read-Discuss

The Listen-Read-Discuss strategy (Manzo and Casale, 1985) is a guided, step-by-step method of using multiple modalities to strengthen students' comprehension of expository text.

Step 1: Listen—First present a brief oral summary of the material.

Step 2: Read—Allow students to read the material, either with partners or by themselves.

Step 3: Discuss—When they have finished, have students set the reading aside. Ask these questions:

- ◆ "What did you understand about what you just read?"

- ◆ "What didn't you understand about what you just read?"

- ◆ "What questions do you still have about this subject?"

Strategies: Possible Sentences; Cooperative Listening; Context

✢ Possible Sentences

Try this variation of possible sentences (Moore and Moore, 1986).

1. Introduce vocabulary words and put them on the board.
2. Read the passage aloud to the class.
3. As a whole group, call on students and have them state possible sentences using the vocabulary words. Record their statements on the board or the overhead just as the student speaks them, without regard for accuracy.
4. Immediately reread the passage (or have the students reread the selection independently).
5. Reread the posted statements.
6. Have students correct any sentences that are wrong.
7. Pair the students and ask them to create a chart, drawing, summary, or graphic organizer that includes all the facts. Make photocopies of their work so that each of the partners has a copy.
8. After they have completed that task, ask, "How does this information relate to what we learned [yesterday, last week, last month]?"

✢ Cooperative Listening

Have students listen to a class presentation. Then put them into groups of three and hand each group two separate sheets. One sheet has questions about the material presented. The other sheet has the answers. Each answer can be used once or not at all. Each team of students works together to match them up. The students will receive a group grade for their effort.

When you prepare this activity, have one more answer than the number of questions (one won't be used) and do not put the answers in the same order as the questions. After you've seen a short film or presented an introduction to energy, you could use this. (**Answers:** 1—c, 2—a, 3—e, 4—b)

Questions (on one sheet)	Answers (on a different sheet)
1. Our bodies get energy from 2. Plants get energy from 3. Most cars get energy from 4. A TV gets energy from	a. sunshine b. electricity c. food d. wind e. gasoline

✢ Listening for Context

This idea helps students to anticipate text, reinforces good listening skills, and provides an effective time filler. Prepare on separate slips cloze sentences from an expository passage the class has already heard or read. Be sure that there is enough context in the sentence to make the answer somewhat obvious. Place all of the slips of paper into a cookie jar or other container. You draw from the jar and read the selected sentence aloud to the class, substituting "hmmm . . ." for the blank. Ask closed-ended statements (see example 1) or open-ended statements (see example 2) and see how many different correct responses you can get:

1. *Hmmm . . .* coloring is an example of an adaptation. *(camouflage)*
2. A rabbit is an example of *hmmm. . . . (a mammal, a vertebrate, a warm-blooded animal, an organism, a rodent, etc.)*

Strategies: Balancing Bar

✛ Main Idea and Supporting Details: Balancing Bar

Students need to determine the main idea and supporting details while listening. It may help to imagine the main idea as a bar balanced on a top of a column. The column (details) holds up (supports) the main idea. Without the column, the bar would fall—just as without details, the main idea is merely a statement without proof. You can illustrate this for students by laying a ruler across the top of an empty juice can. When you remove the juice can, the ruler falls. The balancing bar graphic organizer on page 39 shows children the connection between the main idea and its supporting details. For example:

Water gets polluted in many ways. Factories dump waste into rivers. After it rains, water carries dirt into streams. When you take a bath or wash dishes or clothes, used water goes down the drain. The same is true when you flush a toilet. Used water is called sewage.

Main idea: Water gets polluted in many ways.

Details:

factories dump waste

rainwater

bathwater

dishwater

laundry

toilets

Strategies: Balancing Bar (cont.)

Graphic Organizer

Main idea:

Details:

Strategies: Umbrella

✤ Main Idea and Supporting Details: Umbrella Organizer

Use the umbrella graphic organizer (Jacobson and Raymer, 1999) on page 41 to show your students details covering the main idea. If you need more sections for details, draw additional lines on the graphic organizer before photocopying.

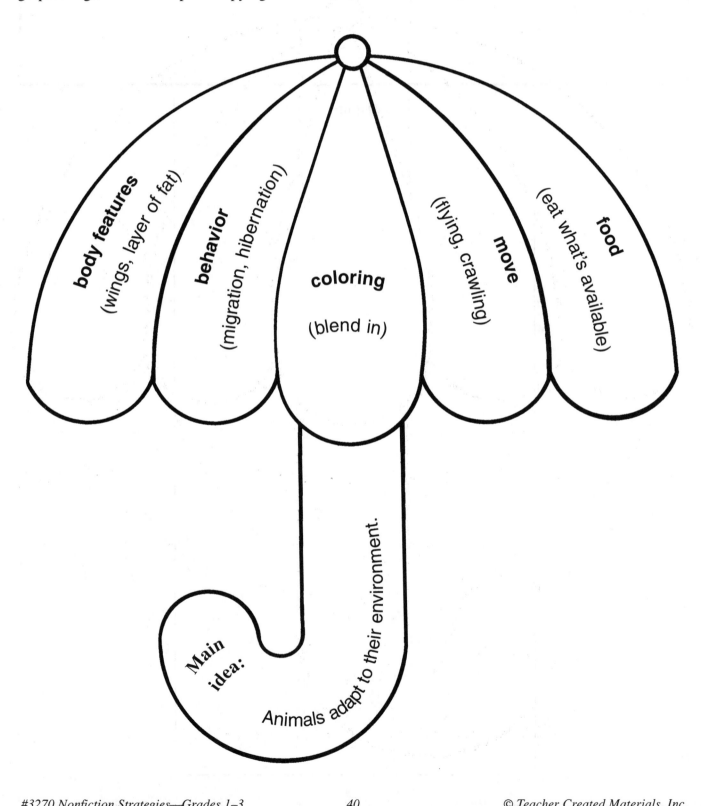

body features (wings, layer of fat)

behavior (migration, hibernation)

coloring (blend in)

move (flying, crawling)

food (eat what's available)

Main idea: Animals adapt to their environment.

Strategies: Umbrella (cont.)

Graphic Organizer

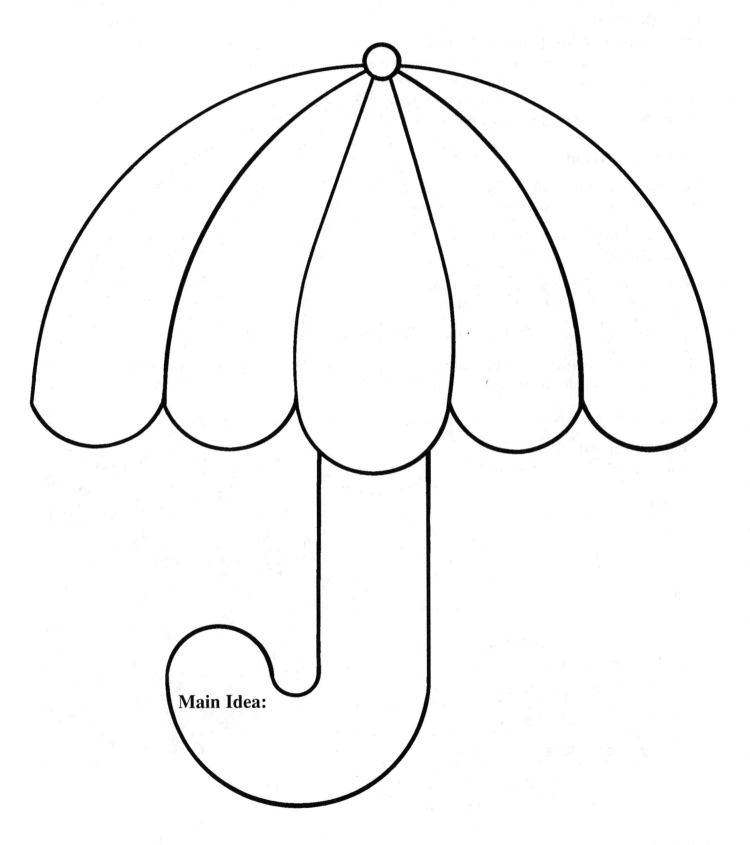

Main Idea:

Strategies: Film Discussion; Listening Guide

✣ Film Discussion

View a film and determine four or five good stopping points. Then put students into groups of three. Give each group member a number 1–3. Show a portion of the film. Stop at the first predetermined stopping point. The students have three minutes in which to discuss the portion of the film just shown. To begin, student #1 will be in charge of recording what the group feels is the key idea. Continue in this manner, rotating the job of scribe to the next student every time you stop the film.

✣ Listening Guide

A Listening Guide (Castallo, 1976) can help students attend to the important points during a film or television show. Here are the steps in this strategy:

1. First, listen to the information yourself, taking notes in the order in which the information is presented.

2. Create a simple, straightforward outline like the one shown below. Leave blank lines where you want students to fill in the information.

3. Photocopy and distribute to the students the outline you've created.

4. Read through it with them. Explain to the students that when they hear the words directly above the lines, the information they need to write on the lines will immediately follow.

In the example shown here, the underlined words were filled in by the students as they listened.

Kinds of Precipitation

rain
_____

fog/mist
_____

snow
_____

freezing rain
_____

sleet
_____

hail
_____

How Much Precipitation

daily in rain forests
_____

almost never in deserts
_____

drought means less than normal
_____

Strategies: Listening/Viewing Guide

✣ Collaborative Listening/Viewing Guide

The Collaborative Listening/Viewing Guide (Wood, et al., 1992) has five steps:

1. Give a preview of an upcoming presentation (such as a slide presentation, videotape, television show, or guest speaker) while your students listen.

2. Have students note key words and important ideas that they hear during the presentation.

3. Have students get together with partners immediately and use what they heard to create a mind map or to answer questions you pose.

4. Synthesize by having the whole class reconvene to discuss (and, if necessary, add to) their mind maps or answers.

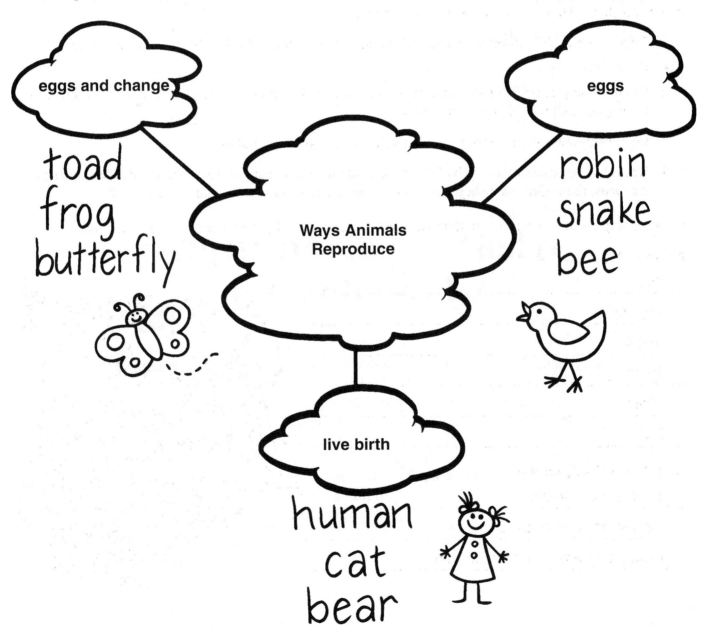

Introduction to Section 3: Discussing Nonfiction

Class discussions are critical to students' development of thinking skills. Listening to each other's ideas lets them consider completely new sets of meanings and introduces them to different viewpoints. Discussions help students to develop stronger reasoning skills by identifying problems, debating about solutions or alternatives, and predicting the consequences of the alternatives. Discussions provide students with practice in these important social skills:

- taking turns

- encouraging others to participate

- valuing each other's ideas

- disagreeing with an idea without attacking the person who proposed it

- giving another group member full attention when he or she is speaking

- using others' ideas as a springboard for their own

- not dominating the discussion

Since students need experience with both whole-group and small-group discussions, the strategies listed in this section are divided into whole group and small group methods.

Whole Group Strategies: Class Observer

✛ Class Observer

Class discussions should involve every child, so don't let one or a few students commandeer a discussion. Call on reticent pupils by name and ask what they think. Control students who tend to dominate class discussions by occasionally putting them in the role of "observer." Tell the observer that you need some help to come up with a discussion grade for the students in class. The observer does not participate in the discussion; instead, he or she keeps track of who does the talking. Hand the student a class list and ask him or her to make a check mark next to the name each time a classmate speaks. This is a subtle way to make the student aware of the fact that some of his or her peers say a lot more than others and to consider his or her own behavior in future discussions.

Whole Group Strategies: List-Group-Label

✢ List-Group-Label

You can use a list-group-label activity (Tierney, Readence, and Dishner, 1990) to develop your students' conceptual knowledge. Give the students a topic and let them brainstorm everything they can think of that relates in any way to the concept in a two-minute time frame. Do not judge any suggestion; record them all. You may be amazed at how many suggestions the students can generate because they are stimulated by their classmates' ideas. Post the list and give a category. Ask the students to find three words on the list that fit the category. Have them do this for as many groups as possible in 10 minutes.

Make sure that your students understand these rules:

- ✦ Terms can be used more than once.
- ✦ Some terms may not fit into any category.
- ✦ The label does not need to come from the list.
- ✦ Only because you are trying to build conceptual connections, the commonality should not be, for example, "words that end in *e*" or "words that begin with *m*" or "words with a short vowel sound."

Example: Brainstorm every word you can think of related to transportation:

car	helicopter	taxi	parking lot	ship
roads	bridge	ferry	van	tunnel
parking meter	truck	toll booth	bicycle	train
train station	fly	highway	token	airport
drive	mail	plane	wheels	jet
streets	railroad crossing	turnpike	submarine	bus
engine	expressway	bus station	railroad tracks	exit
subway	onramp	canals	subway station	fuel
ambulance	people	parking garage	space shuttle	ride
runway	road signs	steering wheel	traffic light	walk

There are many possible sets. Here are just a few:

- **carry people in a city**—bus, subway, taxi
- **make vehicles move**—wheels, engine, fuel
- **move big things**—truck, train, ship
- **move in water**—submarine, ship, ferry
- **move over ground**—truck, car, van
- **parts of an expressway**—onramp, exit, road signs
- **where cars are stopped**—traffic light, parking garage, parking lot
- **things that fly**—plane, helicopter, jet
- **paying for transportation**—toll booth, parking meter, token
- **ways to cross water**—ferry, bridge, tunnel
- **routes**—streets, canals, roads
- **things at an airport**—runway, plane, jet
- **parts of the railroad**—railroad tracks, railroad crossing, train station

Whole-Group Strategies: Semantic Matrix

❖ Semantic Matrix

A semantic matrix (Johnson and Pearson, 1984) should be done after students have had experience with list-group-label categorization. A semantic matrix works best with sets of concrete, familiar things. The matrix helps students establish generalizations. Generalizations enable them to:

- ✦ remember properties and connect them to related items (a student who knows a turtle relates it to a new creature—such as a tortoise)

- ✦ recognize new examples (the student thinks that the tortoise may be a kind of turtle)

- ✦ predict attributes of new examples (the student knows that turtles lay eggs and assumes that tortoises do, too)

Some of the words in the matrix must be familiar to the students so that they have a frame of reference. Fill in as much of the chart as you can prior to reading. If you know that the article will cover the information, do not tell the class if they fill in a slot incorrectly. For this example, suppose you are going to be teaching about reptiles. You believe that many of your students are not familiar with iguanas or tortoises but are familiar with rattlesnakes and snapping turtles. On a blank copy of page 47, set up your chart using both the new concepts and related words that are everyday concepts for your students. Distribute copies to the class and fill in the chart with:

+ (for *yes*)   – (for *no*)   ? (for *don't know*)

Reptile	Cold blooded	Lays eggs	Has scales	Has a shell	Carnivore	Lives in water
iguana	+	+	+	–	?	?
rattlesnake	+	+	+	–	+	–
snapping turtle	+	+	?	+	+	+
tortoise	+	+	?	+	?	?

The question marks set the purpose for reading. Stop whenever you encounter information in the passage that will eliminate a question mark or correct misconceptions (in this case, you'd need to change the information about the rattlesnake eggs). Question marks that remain after reading give you a chance to model how to find the answer by consulting other resources. If no question marks remain, ask your students to complete this generalization:

All reptiles _____. *(are cold blooded and have scales)*

Semantic matrix charts help students to evaluate and differentiate between things in an important way. For example, they may never have realized that although the vast majority of reptiles hatch from eggs, most rattlesnake species give birth to live young.

Whole-Group Strategies:
Semantic Matrix *(cont.)*

Graphic Organizer

Directions: Fill out the chart using the following symbols:

+ (yes)   – (no)   ? (don't know)

Whole-Group Strategies: Venn Diagram

✢ Venn Diagram

Venn diagrams have long been popular for their ability to help students discern similarities and differences.

You can visually demonstrate how a Venn diagram works by displaying an overhead of page 49. Place a yellow transparent circle over one circle. Explain what this circle represents. Remove the yellow circle. Next, place a blue transparent circle over the other circle. Explain what this circle represents. Now put the yellow transparent circle back down. The intersection of the two circles will be green. Just as the color green is part yellow and part blue, the information in the intersection of the circles is a part of both circles.

For example: Ask your students to analyze the numbers 0–9. Prominently display the numbers for the class to see. Starting with zero, fill in the Venn diagram together, discussing where each number goes.

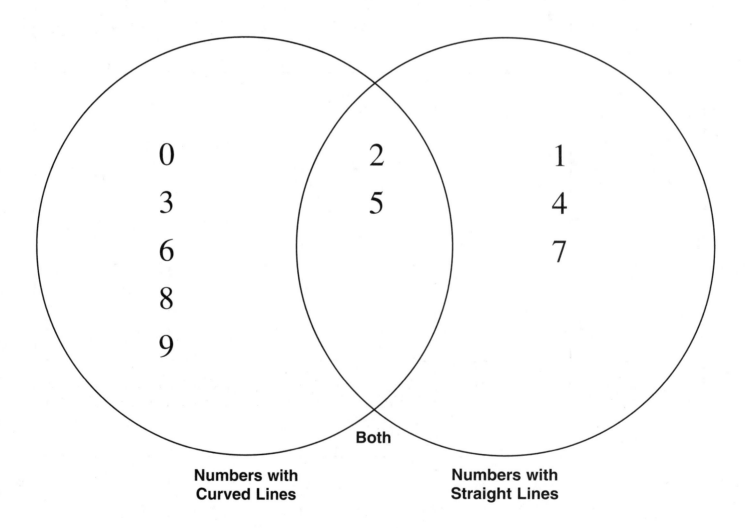

Whole-Group Strategies:
Venn Diagram *(cont.)*

Graphic Organizer

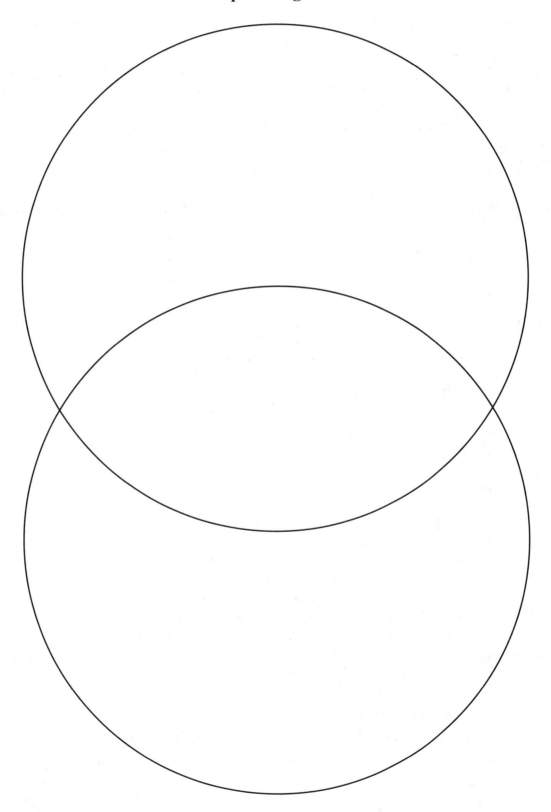

Whole-Group Strategies: Discussing Emotions; Taking a Stand

❖ Discussing Emotions

Emotions are the most personal way to connect to text. Students have a better understanding and retain more information when they try to empathize with those who lived through an event. For example, if you are reading about the Pilgrims' decision to come to America, help your students to understand the emotional ramifications of the situation by asking questions like the following:

♦ How would you feel if you could not worship the way that you want to?

♦ Has anyone ever disliked you because of what you believe? because of how you look or dress? How did you feel when that happened?

♦ What feelings would you have about going on a voyage across the big, stormy Atlantic Ocean? (Show them how far Plymouth, Massachusetts, is from England—over 2,500 miles.)

♦ What would you want to take with you to the New World?

♦ Could you carry those items on a ship?

♦ How would you feel about leaving your home?

♦ Would you be afraid any of your family members would not survive the difficult journey?

♦ Would you be afraid that you wouldn't make it?

♦ What feelings would you have about the new place where you are going to live? (You've never been there before; you just know that it is a wilderness.)

❖ Taking a Stand

When you study an issue that has two sides, post a sign on one side of the room stating one stance and a sign on the opposite wall stating the opposing stance. On the wall in the back, post a sign labeled "Undecided." Have students select a sign to stand beneath. Do not reveal your own opinion; students may be swayed. Students take turns holding a "talking stick" and explaining their beliefs and opinions. Students may change their positions in the horseshoe if they are persuaded by a classmate's arguments. Anyone who speaks without holding the stick must sit down. Students must wait until a speaker signals that he or she is done before raising their hands to get the stick. Each speaker must pass the stick to a student who holds the opposing view or who is undecided. Students will gain an appreciation for debate and enjoy the challenge of trying to persuade their peers to come to their side of the horseshoe.

Whole-Group Strategies: Questioning the Author

✦ Questioning the Author

The Questioning the Author strategy (Beck, et al., 1997) encourages students to take an active, questioning attitude as they cooperatively build meaning from a text. During the discussion, the teacher guides the class through queries.

Traditionally, classroom questions have find-it-stated-in-the-text answers. Since such questions do not require students to analyze information, few remember what they have read. In contrast, queries require students to process information. Students taught through the use of queries tend to readily transfer knowledge across texts and content areas. Queries also make struggling readers less resistant to reading nonfiction.

Traditional Questions	Questioning-the-Author Queries
Students find answers in the text and repeat the author's words to state the answer.	Students have to think about the information and respond in their own words.
Students view the text as an infallible place to find correct answers.	Students view the test as a reference for correct answers.
Mostly teacher-to-students interactions	More student-to-student interaction

Follow these steps for a Questioning the Author lesson:

1. Arrange the classroom desks into a u-shape so that students can easily interact.

2. Plan the Questioning the Author lesson by reading the text to determine for yourself the major concepts you want students to understand. Anticipate and plan for potential problems by predicting how the ideas in the text might be interpreted (or misinterpreted).

3. Segment the text by deciding on specific stopping points where you will initiate queries and class discussion. Establish queries for each segment. Queries should be open-ended and put the onus for developing understanding on the students. Typical queries are as follows:

   - What does the writer mean by _____?
   - What is the writer thinking?
   - What is the writer saying?
   - Why does the writer tell us this?
   - Does the writer explain this clearly?
   - Does this agree with what we read before?
   - How does this connect with what the writer has already said?
   - Why do you think the writer chose to include this?
   - What does the writer expect that we already know?

4. Read the text aloud to the students, stopping at the designated points to pose queries and guide student discussion. You may want to reiterate key points from a student's contribution in a different way (in case someone in the class didn't understand). If your students appear to be missing a key point or seem incapable of grasping an idea, make the point by modeling it as your own thinking: "The author is saying that the colonists were very afraid of minor injuries. Maybe it's because they didn't have antibiotics back then. Without antibiotics even minor cuts that got infected could have killed them."

Whole-Group Strategies: Discussion Prompts

✣ Discussion Prompts

After reading or listening to nonfiction material, choose a set of prompts (Zarnowski, 1998) appropriate for the passage and use them in a whole-class discussion.

What is the main idea? What are the supporting details?

- ✦ What did you do to find the main idea? the supporting details?
- ✦ What's the difference between the main idea and its supporting details?
- ✦ How are the things, people, or events connected?
- ✦ What caused _____ ?
- ✦ What were the consequences of _____ ?
- ✦ How can we summarize this passage?

What are the facts?

- ✦ How do we know which statements are facts?
- ✦ What facts does the author provide in the article?
- ✦ Does the author take a guess or make a prediction? What is it?
- ✦ Does the author say that he or she is certain?

Why did the author write this?

- ✦ Do you agree with the author?
- ✦ What do you disagree with the author about?
- ✦ What would you like to ask the author?
- ✦ What does the author want us remember?

What's the value in knowing history?

- ✦ What is the value of knowing this information?
- ✦ Does it help us to understand another time or place?
- ✦ Does it help to us to understand related events?
- ✦ Does this remind you of anything else that we've studied?
- ✦ Could something similar happen to you or to someone you love?
- ✦ How does this apply to you today?

How can we better understand a historical figure?

- ✦ What difficulties did he or she face?
- ✦ What brought about these challenges?
- ✦ What did he or she do to overcome the problems?

Whole-Group Strategies: Question Exchange

✛ Question Exchange

Question exchanges help students review information. Each student prepares two questions and answers for homework. Each student then poses a question to a classmate in round-robin fashion. If the classmate's answer is incorrect, the first student asks another student for the answer. If the answer is correct, that student asks a question of another. Students should try to ask one of their questions that has not already been asked; however, if necessary, they may repeat one. At the end of the exchange, each student knows the answers to his or her original questions plus the answers to all those questions presented in class. Here's how it works:

Alicia: (*to Benito*) "What five things do people need in order to live?"

Benito: "Air, water, food, shelter, and clothing."

Alicia: "Right."

Benito: (*to Christa*) "Why do people need clothes?"

Christa: "To look good."

Benito: "No, people choose their clothes to look good, but that's not why they need them."

Benito: (*to Damon*) "Why do people need clothes?"

Damon: "Because people would make fun of them if they were naked."

Benito: "People would probably laugh at them, but that's not why people need clothing."

Benito: (*to Elaine*) "Why do people need clothes?"

Elaine: "To protect them from the weather—like cold, rain, and too much sun."

Small-Group Strategies

Today many people are working in teams in the workplace. Therefore, students need experience in working with others. They also need instruction in the social skills listed in the introduction on page 44. They must demonstrate these skills during their interactions with their teammates. To ensure success, adhere to the essential components of small cooperative group instruction:

1. Groups work best with three to four heterogeneous students. For a team of three, that means one high-performing student, one average student, and one low-performing student. In a team of four, two of the students would be average. Do not enlarge the teams: the fewer the group members, the more each individual participates.

2. Your students need to know that the group members need each other. The success of each relies upon the success of all.

3. Everyone must do his or her share by demonstrating personal knowledge of the materials and helping teammates.

4. Provide enough time for lots of interaction among teammates.

5. While your students are working in small groups, facilitate by doing the following:
   - ✦ ensuring that each member does a specific task (or a portion of the overall task)
   - ✦ having students adopt roles such as facilitator, scribe, and timekeeper
   - ✦ providing only one set of materials to each group to encourage interaction
   - ✦ requiring that students talk quietly to keep the noise level to a minimum
   - ✦ circulating among the groups, offering encouragement, resolving disputes, and guiding students in the formation of essential interpersonal skills.

Small-Group Strategies: Why? Pie

❖ Why? Pie

The Why? Pie strategy (Bromley, et al., 1999) encourages students to ask higher level thinking questions in order to establish relationships between concepts. Model the strategy by reading aloud an expository passage as they follow along in their texts. When you are finished, have the students work in pairs to formulate three questions that begin with the word "why" and can only be answered by inference (the answer is not directly stated in the article). In each section of the graphic organizer on page 55, the students write a question stimulated by the text that he or she would like answered. Then they discuss possible responses to their questions. After that, they exchange questions with another pair and develop responses to those questions as well.

You can review the Why? Pies with the class or use them to determine what you want to cover in the next lesson. They can also provide the basis for a class inquiry project (see Researching Nonfiction section). Here's an example of a student's Why? Pie after following along as the teacher read this illustrated article:

America has symbols. When people see these symbols, they think of America. The Liberty Bell is the oldest. It rang on July 4, 1776. On that date, Americans said that they were free from British rules. The Bell is in Philadelphia, Pennsylvania. The American flag is another symbol. It has stars and stripes. There is one star for each state. There is one stripe for each of the first 13 states. The American bald eagle is a symbol because it is beautiful, strong, and lives a long time. The Statue of Liberty is a symbol, too. It stands on Liberty Island in New York. It welcomes people to our great nation.

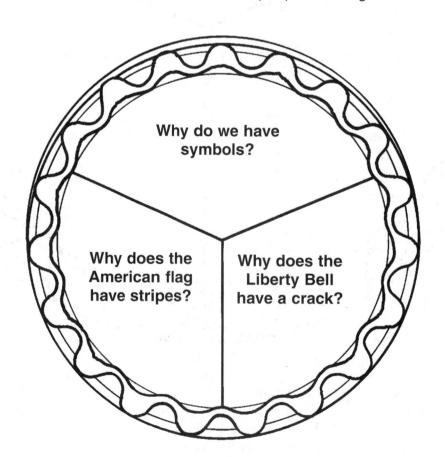

Small-Group Strategies: Why? Pie (cont.)

Graphic Organizer

Small Group Strategies: Brainstorming Carousel; Readers' Guild; Roundtable Discussions

✛ Brainstorming Carousel

Toward the end of a unit, try a brainstorming carousel by posting five sheets of chart or butcher paper around the room. On each sheet, put a simple question: Who? Did What? When? Where? Why? Put the students into five groups and assign each group to one of the question sheets. Each group has two minutes to write its ideas for its question on the sheet before it rotates clockwise to the next question sheet. Then each group has three minutes to read what has already been written on the sheet and add its own unique contributions. This continues until the groups have rotated through all five questions. For example, after studying Christopher Columbus' historic voyage, the first group that stands in front of the "who" sheet writes "Christopher Columbus." Then the second group reads what has been written and adds "Queen Isabella and King Ferdinand" to the same sheet. After that, the third group reads the sheet and decides to write "sailors" on the page, while the fourth group adds "natives." The fifth group puts the "Taino tribe."

✛ Readers' Guild

Establish an extracurricular group where students read about a specified nonfiction topic and come ready to discuss it at a monthly meeting. This provides a valuable way for students to interact across grade levels. Ask the librarian to display a set of relevant nonfiction books in a specified area of the library to make it easy for students who participate in Readers' Guild to select a book quickly.

✛ Roundtable Discussions

During roundtable discussions (Parker, 2001) one student takes the role of the facilitator. He or she keeps the discussion moving and makes sure that everyone has an opportunity to talk. Another student takes the role of scribe and records important points.

The facilitator states the topic and his or her opinion. The discussion moves around the table clockwise, with each student doing the same. Students must listen courteously, disagree appropriately, and ask questions for clarification.

Roundtable discussions are particularly effective for:

- ◆ planning a major class activity (such as organizing a play or puppet show)

- ◆ debating a school or community issue (such as, "How can we help those in our city who are handicapped?") As a follow up, list the options and have the class vote on what they want to do.

Introduction to Section 4: Emerging Reading and Writing Skills

The ability to read well and write well is intertwined. Everything that your students read enhances the development of their writing skills, and everything that your students compose improves their reading skills. Just keep in mind the process of vocabulary acquisition:

Stage 1: The student hears a new word spoken in context:

The *enormous* fire destroyed six buildings.

Stage 2: The student reads the same word in print:

The ship was lost during an *enormous* storm.

State 3: The student uses the word in an appropriate context when speaking:

The Toronto Zoo is *enormous*.

Stage 4: The student uses the word in his or her own written composition:

Most dinosaurs were *enormous*.

Strategies: Word Walls

✛ **Word Walls**

Students learn about print by seeing print—the more, the better. Therefore, use black marker on fluorescent note cards to label objects around the room. Then every time that a student looks at an object (such as a bookshelf), the first thing that catches his or her eye is the object's name.
Post content area vocabulary, high-frequency words, and spelling demons on a classroom wall.
Encourage the students to consistently use the wall as a resource whenever they are reading or writing.

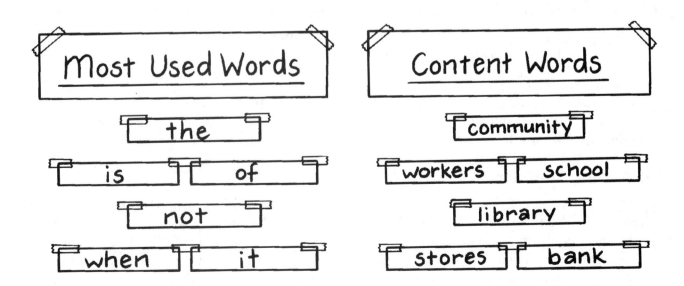

Strategies: Word Choices; Decoding; Phonemic Awareness

✢ Expanding Word Choices

Students who use a variety of words in their writing have the most interesting compositions. In order to use a lot of words, students must know a lot of words. Expand their vocabulary with this activity:

1. Write a word on the board (for example, *break*).
2. See how many synonyms the class can generate in two minutes. Record the list of synonyms on chart paper. In this case, the students came up with *smash*, *wreck*, *crack*, *bust*, *ruin*, and *destroy*.
3. Next, give the students two minutes to think of antonyms for the word. Record the list of antonyms on another piece of chart paper. In this example, the students thought of *repair*, *fix*, *put together*, *mend*, and *make better*.
4. Post the class lists on a word wall and encourage the students to use the words in an appropriate writing assignment. After posting the class lists, your students will have seven ways to express "break" and five ways to express "fix" in future compositions.

✢ Decoding With Confidence

Learning the rules of phonics and spelling is most meaningful when taught within the context of genuine texts. It's wise to introduce the concepts in this sequence:

1. Consonant sounds (teach *Q* as *qu*)
2. Short vowel sounds. Post this sentence and refer to it frequently: Jack Dylan is not up yet. It demonstrates all the short vowel sounds. It also shows *y* as both a vowel (most often) and a consonant (usually only when it's the first letter of a word).
3. Consonant digraphs (*th*, *sh*, *ch*, *wh*, *ph*)
4. Long vowel sounds due to magic *e*
5. Consonant blends (*sc*, *sk*, *st*, *sl*, *br*, *bl*, *fl*, *fr*, etc.)
6. The long vowel sound of *y* at the end of a word (usually says *ee*; in one syllable words says *i*)
7. Vowel digraphs ("Two vowels walking, the first one does the talking.")
8. Vowel diphthongs (vowels that violate the digraphs rule: *ou*, *ow*, *au*, *aw*, *oi*, *oy*, *oo*)
9. Consonant trigraphs (*thr*, *shr*, *sch*, etc.)
10. R-controlled vowels (*ar*, *er*, *ir*, *or*, *ur*). Present these words and have the students read them: *had*, *gem*, *bid*, *pot*, and *hut*. Then say, "Rowdy R pushes his way in right before the final letter. What does the word say now?" (Answers: *hard*, *germ*, *bird*, *port*, and *hurt*)

✢ Phonemic Awareness Games

Play games using content area vocabulary: "Who can think of a word that begins with the same sound as walrus?" or "Who can think of a word that rhymes with rain?" Another phonetic game is "I Spy." Show the class an illustration in a nonfiction big book or picture book and say, "I spy something that begins with the *f* sound. (If you want the students to correctly identify sounds, and a student says *f* for the beginning sound of *phone*, the answer should be accepted.)

Strategies: Unlock the Meaning; Word Parts

✢ Unlock the Meanings of New Words

Emergent readers rely heavily on picture clues. As they gain more reading skill, they gradually move to context clues. You can encourage this process by thinking aloud about your own thought processes when using context to determine word meaning. Once you've done enough think-alouds for the class to feel comfortable, invite volunteers to do their own think-alouds for their classmates. This lets poor readers experience the thought processes of successful peers. Students can learn a great deal about text processing from each other.

Even with picture and context clues, young readers benefit from an understanding of common word parts to unlock the meanings of new words. Introduce the concept of affixes by giving examples of a few from the chart below. Ask students to suggest any that they know. This will help you to determine if there are any that you will not need to spend time studying.

When teaching prefixes and suffixes, it is wise to give the students a group of words that they already know, such as *eating*, *talking*, *walking*, and *crying*. Tell your students they are word detectives. Ask them to identify the common letters in all the words (ing). Explain that this is a word ending for many words. Have the class think about what the words mean. Ask for volunteers to give you definitions. Write these on the board. Ask the students if they can detect what the word part means (-ing = doing an action).

Teach students to cover affixes as soon as they recognize them, so that they can concentrate on the base word. Next, they should uncover the prefix, then the suffix, and finally put the word together. Be alert to opportunities of pointing out words with affixes in a wide variety of places (on the Internet, during the announcements, or during a video or television show).

✢ Important English Word Parts for Primary Grades

Prefix	Meaning	Example
un	not	undo
re	again	resend
in, im	not	impossible
dis	opposite	dislike
non	not	nonfiction
over	too much	overheat
mis	bad	misunderstood
pre	before	preview
de	opposite	defrost
under	less	undercook

Suffix	Meaning	Example
-s or -es	more than one	bats; heroes
-ed	did an action	packed
-ing	doing an action	going
-ly	like, every	really
-er	a person who	teacher
-ful	full of	beautiful
-or	a person who	editor
-less	without	fearless
-er	more	sadder
-est	most	saddest

From White, T., et al., (1989) "Teaching Elementary Students to Use Word-Part Clues."
The Reading Teacher, 42, 302–309.

Strategies: Stages of Spelling and Writing

✤ Developmental Stages of Spelling and Writing

Since writing is learned best through writing, editing, and rewriting, encourage your students to write every day. Spelling and writing skills develop in a nonlinear fashion; most children fluctuate between two stages, depending upon the complexity of the writing task. Each child moves through the stages at his or her own pace. One first grader may struggle to attain stage 8 by the end of the year while another reaches stage 11 midyear. For many students, stages 13 and 14 may not be accomplished until the end of third grade or later.

Stage	Expect to See	Example (using elephant)
1	random letters to represent words	mptr (for *elephant*)
2	the initial consonant sound of the word	l
3	The initial consonant and one other consonant—usually the final consonant sound; spaces appear between some words	lt
4	letters that phonetically match the dominant sounds in the word	lfnt
5	a vowel (often an *e* or an *a*) as a marker for all vowel sounds	lafant
6	vowel sounds in a word—starting with the long vowel sounds (because they say their names)	lefunt
7	inventive spelling close to conventional spelling; frequent substitutions include *r* for vowel sounds and *f* for *th* sounds	elefant
8	*familiar* sight words spelled correctly	a big elefant
9	short, simple sentences	a elefant is big.
10	consonant digraphs in words (th, sh, ch, ph, wh)	elephant
11	a group of two to four sentences sequenced to form a basic paragraph, although terminal punctuation may be mostly absent	A elephant is big it has a trunk. it rechs for food with its trunk a elephant baby is a caf.
12	vowel digraphs appear in compositions—however, they may not be used correctly (such as *oo* for *ow*)	A coo is a girl elephant.
13	more consistent use of basic mechanics, such as a period at the end of a sentence and capitalization of the first word in a sentence; some grammar and spelling are still incorrect	A elephant is big. It has a trunk. It rechs for food with the trunk. a coo is a girl elephant. A elephant baby is a calf.
14	a first draft that concentrates on content and a revised, final draft that exhibits proper grammar, spelling, and mechanics; longer sentences and overall composition	An elephant is big. It has a trunk. It reaches for its food with the trunk. A cow is a female elephant. It has a baby calf. The cow takes care of the calf for two years. Then it can take care of itself.

Strategies: Stages of Spelling and Writing; Sentence Frames; Game

So that anyone can understand a composition even after the passage of time, ask the students if you can print the words beneath the invented spellings of a passage. If they agree, use tiny lettering under only the words that cannot be readily deciphered.

With beginning writers, do not correct the spelling, terminal punctuation, or capitalization. Later in the year, after you've covered these topics, revisit earlier compositions and let the children correct their own documents. They will get a kick out of reading their old pieces and seeing their own growth.

Always respond primarily to the meaning of writing. Give specific praise like, "Your writing made me see an elephant calf standing beside its mother. That's what good writing does—it helps the readers form pictures in their minds." After this initial praise, mention something that the student can easily improve upon such as, "Everytime you write the word 'I' all by itself, it needs to be a capital 'I.' Can you find all the lonely I's in this passage and make them into capitals?"

During first grade expect invented spellings with only sight words spelled correctly. By the middle of second grade most students misspell about one-third of all words in a piece. At the end of third grade, the average student will misspell no more than 10 percent of all words in a piece.

✛ Sentence Frames

Have students fill in factual statements by completing sound boxes in sentence frames, like this:

The Mayflower was a ☐ ☐ ☐ ☐ .

Thomas Edison made the ☐ ☐ ☐ ☐ ☐ light bulb.

Omit words that can be readily sounded out (*ship*) or sight words necessary to the meaning of the sentence (*first*). The latter meets two objectives simultaneously: teaching children to rely on context and using phonics to figure out how to spell words.

✛ Sentence-Building Game

Primary students use choppy, three- or four-word sentences. Use this fun activity to improve their ability to compose longer sentences. Pair the students and give them a simple sentence. Ask the partners to take turns adding words to the sentence to lengthen it. Eliminate the task of printing the words by letting the students use a word processor or magnetic words. Suppose you gave a pair the following sentence: "I went shopping." Here are some possible responses:

1st-grade pair's final sentence: "I went shopping with Mom today."

2nd-grade pair's final sentence: "I went shopping for a new pair of jeans yesterday."

3rd-grade pair's final sentence: "I went shopping with Mom while Dad watched the football game."

Strategies: Stages in Report Writing

✧ Developmental Stages in Nonfiction Report Writing

There are five developmental stages to writing an independent report in the primary grades. All children's writing skills develop at their own pace, but the first three stages are most frequently seen during kindergarten and grade 1. Second graders' work is usually associated with stage 4, and stage 5 is seen most often in third grade.

Stage 1: The student draws a picture about the topic and dictates the report to an adult.

Stage 2: The student writes a rebus report, using inventive spellings and lots of pictures:

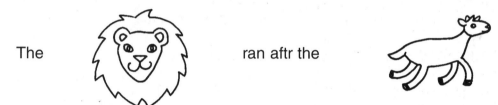

The   ran aftr the   .

Stage 3: The student moves to writing a rebus report with labels beneath the pictures:

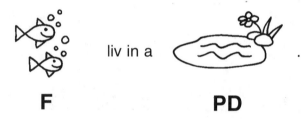

liv in a

F   **PD**

Stage 4: The student stops doing rebuses, substituting one or more detailed illustrations created prior to composing. Child may still use inventive spelling for words other than sight words.

Lions have 2 or 3 cubs. Lions chas antlops. When they catch one, they et it. They chu up the meet so the cubs can et to.

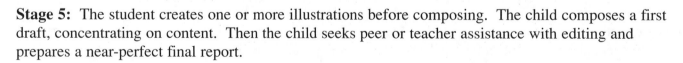

Stage 5: The student creates one or more illustrations before composing. The child composes a first draft, concentrating on content. Then the child seeks peer or teacher assistance with editing and prepares a near-perfect final report.

Lions have two or three cubs. Lions chase antelopes. When they catch one, they eat it. The mother lion chews up the meat for the cubs to eat.

Introduction to Section 5: Reading Nonfiction

Reading is the foundation of all learning, and nonfiction reading comprises the bulk of what students will see and use all of their lives. Therefore, your students must feel comfortable and confident reading expository text. But the skills needed for reading nonfiction are not identical to those used for reading fiction. This means that students need direct instruction, guided practice, and lots of support and encouragement. If you are working with emergent readers, please read the Emerging Reading and Writing Skills section (pages 57–62). Because reading requires so many complex skills, the strategies in this section are grouped in the following order:

- guided reading (beginning with DRTA on this page)
- asking questions before, during, and after reading (page 64)
- envisioning text while reading (page 70)
- finding the main idea and supporting details (beginning on page 71)
- understanding text structure (page 76)
- using signal words to make inferences (page 77)
- time order and sequencing (beginning on page 79)
- comparing/contrasting (beginning on page 82)
- summarizing (beginning on page 84)
- self-monitoring when independently reading nonfiction (page 88)

Strategies: DRTA

✥ Guiding Reading: Directed Reading and Thinking Activity (DRTA)

Use the Directed Reading and Thinking Activity (DRTA) (Stauffer, 1969) to prepare students to learn from expository text. Divide the text to be read into meaningful segments—often a paragraph or two. For each section, follow these steps:

1. **Preview**—Preview the text by calling attention to the headings, illustrations, and graphics. Show students how to actively turn the headings into questions by doing one of the following:
   - ✦ adding a question mark at the end ("Electricity?")
   - ✦ putting "what is" or "what are" in front of the heading ("What is electricity?")
   - ✦ turning the heading into a cloze statement ("Electricity _____ .")

2. **Predict**—Have the students jot a predictions in their learning logs.
   "Electricity comes from outlets in the wall."

3. **Read**—They read to prove or disprove their predictions. The reading may be done by you, chorally with the whole class, or with a partner.

4. **Prove**—After reading, have the students write "true" or "false" next to their prediction. If it is false, ask them to state what they could change to make it true.
   "Electricity must be made. It can be made from burning fuel, falling water, sunshine, or wind."

Strategies: Strategic Questioning; Asking Questions

❖ Guided Reading: Strategic Questioning

Strategic Questioning (King, 1991) enables students to build new knowledge by hearing each other's responses. Questions help students, especially struggling readers, to focus on what's important in a text. When asking questions, remember the significance of wait time. The amount of time you wait for a student to answer after posing a question has a critical effect on learning. So, after you ask a student a question, silently count to five (or ten if you have a student who struggles to put thoughts into words) before giving any additional prompts or redirecting the question to another student. Start by telling the students the title of the passage or book, showing them the front cover or an illustration, and asking:

- ✦ What kind of information do you expect to read?
- ✦ What kind of illustrations do you expect to see?
- ✦ Do you know anything about this topic?

Preview the text by reading the title and italicized or bold print words; skimming any pictures, diagrams, charts, time lines, or graphs and scanning any captions that accompany illustrations.

Next, ask a few questions that seem most appropriate for the specific passage:

- ✦ Which words are emphasized (appear in bold or italic print)?
- ✦ Why do you think the author chose to emphasize those words?
- ✦ What do you think the main idea will be?
- ✦ What graphics (pictures, graphs, charts, and diagrams) are included? How do we read them?
- ✦ Why do you think these particular graphics were included?

If you discover through strategic questioning that your students lack sufficient background knowledge, employ strategies from the Preparing for Nonfiction section.

❖ Asking Questions Before, During, and After Reading

Model reading a passage by stopping and telling your class each question that occurs to you, jotting the question's key words(s) on a sticky-note and placing it in the textbook (Harvey and Goudvis, 2000).

When the text answers one of these questions, press the sticky note in the book's margin and draw a star on it to show that it was answered. When you encounter a passage that confuses you, say "Huh?" and then reread to clarify. If you still don't understand, record a question mark on a sticky note, press it into the book's margin, and read further. When you encounter material that clears up your confusion, move the sticky note with the question mark to the appropriate place in the book's margin and draw a star on it to show that you now understand. If your question remains unanswered after you have completed the passage, form a question on the sticky note and press it onto a sheet of notebook paper. This is a "research question." Tell your students of your plan for finding the answer and then follow through. It impresses students when the teacher cares enough to find an answer.

After modeling this active questioning process, tackle a grade-level text with the whole class, using the same sticky-note technique. Once the students appear to understand the strategy, distribute sticky notes and ask them to code their own nonfiction reading.

Strategies: Headings; ReQuest

✛ Turning Headings into Questions

Students need lots of practice turning a question into a partial statement and then looking for that statement to find the question's answer. When you hand out questions related to a passage, have the students practice turning the questions into statements like this:

Question	Turned into a Statement to Look for in Text
Where is Mount Everest?	Mount Everest is . . .
What is a magnet?	A magnet is . . .
How did the first people come to America?	The first people came to America . . .

✛ ReQuest

Take turns posing and answering questions with ReQuest (Manzo, 1969). Read the passage in advance and determine stopping points where you will ask questions. Read aloud the first part. Stop and let the students ask you a question. Read the next section, and then ask the class a question. Continue taking turns posing and answering questions in this manner. In the following transcript, the italicized words are the text:

What do apples, tomatoes, peaches, plums, and kiwis have in common? Besides the fact that they are all fruits, they all contain vitamin A.

Student A: "Is a tomato really a fruit?"

Teacher: *(to student A)* "Yes. So is a pumpkin. Any fleshy body with seeds inside is considered a fruit. The fleshy part nourishes the seeds as they grow."

Teacher: *(to class)* "What do you think vitamin A is?"

Student A: "A pill."

Student B: "Something that's good for you."

Student C: "Something that makes fruits colorful."

Teacher: "Each of you choose a prediction. Then I'll read on, and we'll see if it's right."

Vitamin A is very important for us. Our bodies and eyes need vitamin A to stay healthy. It may keep us from getting colds and the flu.

Teacher: "Which prediction was the closest?" *(brief discussion)* "What do you think the article will talk about next?"

Strategies: Folded Paper

✛ Folded-Paper Questions and Answers

Write questions that can be answered by the text on the graphic organizer on page 67. Photocopy and distribute to the students. Have the children fold on the vertical line to turn under the answer column. They should see only the question and page number columns. As they read, they should record the page number on which the answers appear. After reading, they lay the paper out flat and fill in the answer column. For those answers they can't recall, they can rely on the page number column to guide them to the information.

Question	Page Number	Answer
How did people buy things before there was money?	346	They traded goods and services with each other.
Which people have their faces on American money?	348	past presidents
Where are American coins made?	349	at the U.S. mint
What piece of money is the most recognized in the world?	349	an American $1 bill

Strategies: Folded Paper *(cont.)*

Graphic Organizer

Question	Page Number	Answer

Strategies: Question-Answer Relationships

❖ Question-Answer Relationships

T. E. Raphael created the Question-Answer Relationships strategy (1984) to help students recognize the kinds of questions frequently asked by textbooks, teachers, and tests and how to locate their answers in a nonfiction text. After the students have read a passage, provide a series of questions on the Question-Answer Relationships graphic organizer on page 69. Explain to the students that there are three kinds of answers:

1. Stated (**S**)—The answer is easy to find because the words used in the questions and the words in the text are identical. (See question #1 in the example below.)

2. Look for it (**L**)—The words used in the passage and the words in the question are different but similar. (See question # 2 in the example below.)

3. Think about it (**T**); not in the passage—The answer requires students to combine the text information with what they know to frame a response. (See question #3 in the example below.)

The students complete the graphic organizer by coding the questions and writing the answers in the spaces provided. This example is based on the following paragraph:

> There are things you can do to stay well. It is important to keep clean. Always wash your hands before eating. Most germs get into your body through your mouth and nose. When you eat, your hands are near your mouth and nose. And you eat many things with your hands.

Codes:

S = the answer was stated

L = you had to look for the answer

T = you thought about it to come up with an answer

Question	Code	Answer
1. How do most germs get into your body?	S	1. They go in my mouth or nose.
2. How can you keep from getting sick?	L	2. By washing my hands before eating.
3. Why do germs make us sick?	T	3. Because they get into our bodies. They should not be inside our bodies.

Strategies: Question-Answer Relationships *(cont.)*

Graphic Organizer

Code each question with one of these letters:

S = the answer was stated

L = you had to look for the answer

T = you thought about it to come up with the answer

Question	Code	Answer
1.		
2.		
3.		
4.		
5.		

Strategies: Envisioning Text

✛ Envisioning Text While Reading

Primary students often depend on pictures to help tell the story. Many nonfiction texts have fewer illustrations than fiction. Therefore, students need to learn new ways of visualizing. Promote these skills through think-alouds that describe your own text visualization. Read aloud the first paragraph of a passage and describe what images come to your mind. Include details that were not stated in the text, such as "the forest floor had splashes of sunlight where the sun filtered through the tree branches and you hear the buzz of insects." Then read further and explain how you modified or added to your image based on the additional information. For example, if later on the text says it was raining, your sun-splashed forest floor would have to change to soggy and dim. The insect sounds would change to the dripping of the falling raindrops.

When you are doing a think-aloud for your class, be sure to do the following:

- ◆ Tell how your mental images relate to the passage's key concepts.
- ◆ Explain how your images help you to better understand the passage.
- ◆ Describe details, being certain to include those that you added from your own schema.
- ◆ Mention the use of your senses—the more the better.
- ◆ Show how the text affected your emotions.
- ◆ Discuss your empathy for the people or creatures in the text.
- ◆ Describe how your mental images change as you read further and gain more information.

When you read a passage containing measurements, find creative ways for students to relate them to things with which they are familiar. Use comparisons that will enable children to envision size or characteristics—for example, "Our hearts are approximately the same size as our fists" and "Muskee teeth are a sharp as razor blades." If a text reads, "A full-grown komodo dragon can weigh 300 pounds and be six feet in length," your students probably cannot imagine those dimensions. So gather together a group of about six students (each weighing 50 pounds) and have them stand in a tight knot in front of the class. Explain that their combined weight is 300 pounds. Have students measure six feet across the chalkboard or on the floor (using masking tape). These simple steps will give students a better idea of the creature's size. For enormous dimensions (such as those of a dinosaur) mark the dimensions with chalk on the school's driveway or parking lot.

Using clues from illustrations, skillful readers imagine the missing pictures that link the illustrations together and make the story flow. Go through a wordless picture book with the class, looking at and discussing the pictures. Ask students to draw what they visualize happening between two of the pictures and write a caption for it (Harvey, 1998).

For example, in David Wiesner's book *Tuesday*, there is a picture of a frog on a flying lily pad being chased by a big dog. In the next illustration, the dog is fleeing from a squadron of frogs on flying lily pads. Ask your students to draw the missing event that must have occurred. Your quick scan of each student's drawing of the missing event (the startled dog turning around when he sees all the frogs coming) will enable you to immediately detect misconceptions so that you can address problems quickly. (You can find other good examples in *Carl's Day at the Park* by Alexandra Day.)

Strategies: GIST

✢ GIST: Finding the Main Idea

Use the GIST: Finding the Main Idea strategy (Cunningham, 1982) to introduce the concept of main idea. Have your students read the first paragraph of a text and then immediately write the main idea in a learning log using a single sentence. The older the student, the more detailed response you can expect. For the youngest students, be pleased when they record any major understanding from the paragraph. For example:

Our Sun and Moon

The sun is at the center of our solar system. It is a big yellow star that gives heat and light to Earth. The sun is so bright that we cannot directly look at it.

Typical main idea responses:

- ◆ *first grader:* The sun gives us heat.

- ◆ *second grader:* The sun is a star that gives Earth light and heat.

- ◆ *third grader:* The sun is the star at the center of the solar system and gives Earth light and heat.

The sun is always shining. We can not see it at night. But it is shining in the sky on the other side of the world. The sun is still there on cloudy days. The clouds just hide it.

Typical main idea responses:

- ◆ *first grader:* The sun always shines.

- ◆ *second grader:* The sun is always there even when we can't see it.

- ◆ *third grader:* The sun shines even at night and on cloudy days.

The moon has no light of its own. It reflects the sun's light. The moon seems to change shape. But it really does not. The whole moon is still there. We just see less of it when part of the moon is in the Earth's shadow. The moon looks round when it is not in the Earth's shadow at all.

Typical main idea responses:

- ◆ *first grader:* The sun lights up the moon.

- ◆ *second grader:* The whole moon is there even when we can only see a part of it.

- ◆ *third grader:* The amount of the moon we can see changes because of the Earth's shadow.

Strategies: Main Idea; Main Street

❖ Identifying the Main Idea and Supporting Details

Learning to identify and focus on the main idea can be difficult for primary students. One way to do this is to ask them to tell the main idea in one breath. You can use the four-step strategy outlined here. Begin with paragraphs in which the main idea is obvious (even if it is not stated in a topic sentence).

> Long ago an animal died. It fell to the ground and mud covered it. Over time, more mud pressed down on it. After a very long time, its bones changed into rock. This rock is called a fossil. Some fossils are millions of years old. When we find a fossil, we see the form of the dead animal's body. Fossils tell us about animals that have died off, like dinosaurs.

Step 1: Identify the key word(s) in each sentence.

1. long ago, animal, died
2. fell, ground, mud, covered
3. mud, pressed down
4. bones, changed, rock
5. rock, fossil
6. fossils, millions of years old
7. fossil, form, dead animal
8. fossils, dinosaurs

Step 2: Identify the topic (what most of the sentences have in common): <u>fossils</u>

Step 3: Write a sentence stating the main idea (based on information from Steps 1 and 2).
<u>We know about animals from millions of years ago because of their fossils.</u>

Step 4: If possible, locate a sentence in the paragraph that states the main idea.
<u>"Fossils tell us about animals that have died off like dinosaurs."</u>

❖ Main Idea and Supporting Details: Main Street Organizer

Using the graphic organizer of a main street with buildings on page 73 is an effective way for students to visually represent the main idea and supporting details. For example:

> In South Dakota there is a special mountain. It is called Mount Rushmore. Four men's heads are carved into its rock. Each head is 60 feet (20 m) tall! It took 14 years for workers to shape these heads. The heads are of George Washington, Thomas Jefferson, Abraham Lincoln, and Theodore Roosevelt. All of these men were U. S. presidents.

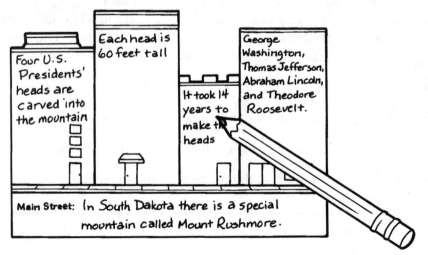

Strategies: Main Street *(cont.)*

Graphic Organizer:

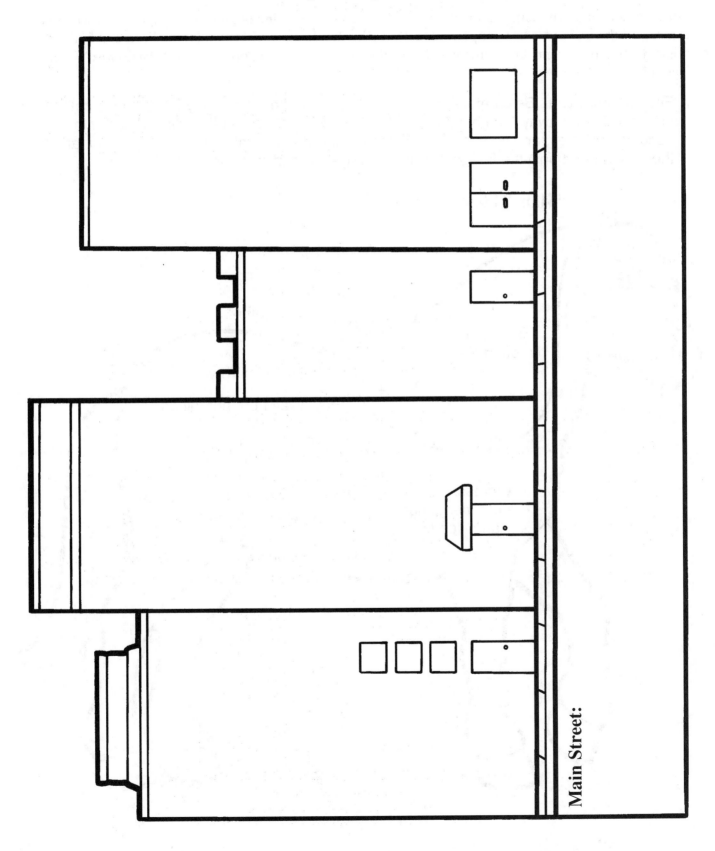

Main Street:

Strategies: Horse Organizer

✛ Main Idea and Supporting Details: Horse Organizer

For those students who enjoy homophones, there is a horse graphic organizer on page 75 on which they can record the main idea and supporting facts. Since the details are written on the head and body of the horse, logic lets students know that the head and body are what supports the mane (main idea). For example:

Fire can burn you. Be careful around fire. Clothes, paper, and many other things catch fire easily. So keep away from hot things like stoves, grills, and heaters. Never play with candles, matches, or a lighter. If you catch on fire, do not run! Drop to the ground, and then roll around until the fire goes out. Then get up and get help.

"Mane" idea:

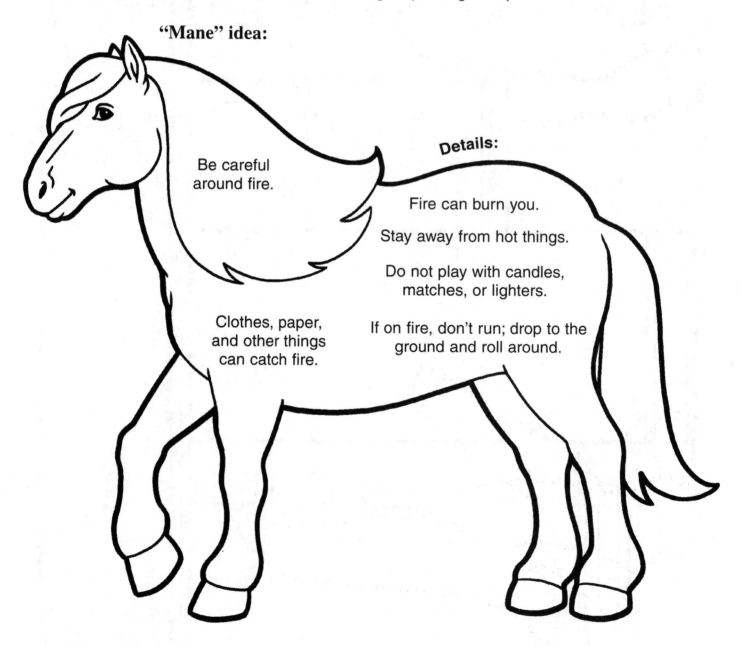

Be careful around fire.

Clothes, paper, and other things can catch fire.

Details:

Fire can burn you.

Stay away from hot things.

Do not play with candles, matches, or lighters.

If on fire, don't run; drop to the ground and roll around.

Strategies: Horse Organizer (cont.)

Graphic Organizer

"Mane" idea:

Details:

Strategies: Inferential Skills; Text Structure

⊹ Teaching Inferential Skills

To achieve success at reading nonfiction materials, your students need to develop inferential skills. Explain to students that authors want readers to use their own experiences and knowledge as they read. They expect readers to "read between the lines" and understand things that are not directly stated. Research has shown the three skills readers need to be successful at inferential comprehension:

1. using text structure to construct meaning
2. realizing that inferences are tentative predictions that must be discarded if new information negates them
3. recognizing words that indicate comparisons, cause and effect relationships, or a sequence of events

⊹ Text Structure

Skillful readers use text structure to construct meaning. Guide your students through a sample text, emphasizing its organization. Model the text structures using a sentence about the concept of "taste," as shown in the last column of the table:

Structure Type	Used To	Common Example	"Taste" Example
description or explanation	define or describe a thing or concept	encyclopedia entry about killer whales	Taste is one of our five senses. Taste buds are tiny bumps on the human tongue that enable taste. Their purpose is to keep us from eating dangerous things.
cause and effect	explain why or how something happens	bumping a vase knocks it off the desk	When I put something in my mouth, my taste buds tell me whether I like it or not.
sequence	tells series of events over a period of time	historical event or order in which things occur (the creation, use, and decline of the Erie Canal)	First the boy chews the food. Then his taste buds send a signal to his brain about how the food tastes.
lists	state items that all have the same importance, often with bullets or numbers	directions on how to hook up a new VCR	The five senses are sight, hearing, touch, smell, and taste.
compare or contrast	show similarities and differences; positives and negatives	similarities and differences between reptiles and amphibians	Unlike our other senses, taste partially depends upon our sense of smell. When we cannot smell (such as when we have a cold), we cannot taste very well.

Nonfiction text structures rarely encountered before fourth grade are not listed in this chart.

Strategies: Signal Words; Cause and Effect

❖ Signal Words

Concentrating on one type at a time, display a simple web with the text structure type in a central circle and the signal words given in the chart below radiating out from it. Use those words that you feel are appropriate for your grade level. Build student awareness by:

♦ asking the students to point out the signal words in the materials you read as a class.

♦ providing the class with sentences and asking them to identify the signal words.

♦ making a word wall or bulletin board that groups the different types of signal words.

♦ putting the students into small groups and having each group create three sentences that include signal words, then asking another group to identify the signal words and what text structure indicate.

These Signal Words	Indicate This Text Structure
since, because, caused by, as a result, before and after, so, this led to, if/then, reasons, brought about, so that, when/then, leading up to, resulting in, that's why	cause and effect The answer to **"Why did it happen?"** is a cause. The answer to **"What happened?"** is an effect.
first, second, third, next, than, after, before, last, later, since then, now, while, meanwhile, at the same time, finally, when, at last, in the end, since that time, following, on (date), at (time)	sequence
but, even if, even though, although, however, instead, not only, unless, yet, on the other hand, either/or, as well as, compared with, related to, in spite of, "-er" and "-st" words (such as better, shorter, tallest, biggest, smallest, most, worst, best, least)	compare/contrast

❖ Teaching Cause and Effect

Prepare the sentence strips on page 78, leaving space at the end of each strip for numbers 1–15. A line shows you where to leave the space on each strip for numbers 16–30. Numbers 1–15 are causes that requires a child to give an effect. Numbers 16–30 are effects that require the child to provide a cause. Underline the clue word(s) as shown. Laminate the strips for durability and post them. Assign each child a number 1–30. Give the children two minutes to draw or write on a rectangular sticky note something that will logically complete his or her statement, then press it on the sentence strip. Each child reads aloud the sentence to the class, including the part he or she contributed. Repeat this activity, having those who did 1–15 last time do 16–30 this time. In this way, every child provides one cause and one effect.

Strategies: Cause and Effect *(cont.)*

Cause and Effect Sentence Strips

1.	Because it was so cold, _____
2.	If your hands are dirty, _____
3.	Since he woke up late, _____
4.	After Kim got a skateboard, _____
5.	When the ball rolled into the street, _____
6.	Since it was raining so hard, _____
7.	Because she left the door open, _____
8.	Since we found the cat, _____
9.	After the fire, _____
10.	Because she lost her shoe, _____
11.	If it rains today, _____
12.	When the dog ran away, _____
13.	Since she forgot to set the timer, _____
14.	Because of the storm, _____
15.	Since he had left the water running, _____
16.	_____ which caused the electricity to go off.
17.	_____ so we won the game.
18.	_____ after that, Jan had to wash the dishes.
19.	_____ the dog growled.
20.	_____ he blew out the candles.
21.	Dan had to stay after school because _____.
22.	_____ that's why Jamie's room was messy.
23.	_____ so Ben lost the race.
24.	_____ then she fixed the flat tire.
25.	Mrs. Bend called the police when _____.
26.	_____ as a result, Tim stayed home.
27.	_____ so she missed the bus.
28.	_____ which made Amy fall.
29.	_____ then Pat owed me a dime.
30.	_____ his friend got mad.

Strategies: Teaching Sequence

✤ Teaching Sequence

Introduce the concept of sequence by creating the sentence strips below and posting them on a pocket chart or board. Read the strips with your class and help them to decide in what order the events probably occurred. Move the strips to show the correct order. Ask the children to identify what happened before noon, after noon, and in the evening.

Leave the strips up. Have your students create an individual time line by asking them to draw pictures of at least six things they did yesterday, then cut and paste them on a piece of construction paper in the order in which they occurred, adding a caption beneath each, such as *I brushed my teeth.*

get home from school	put on pajamas
go to bed	eat breakfast
watch television	school starts
do homework	take a bath
get home from school	eat a snack
play indoors	play outside
eat dinner	eat lunch
get up	comb hair
do chores	get dressed

For the next activity, write each of the following sentences on a sentence strip; use all one color sentence strips for the first example and another color for the second, etc. Post the strips in random order. Guide children to rearrange the strips: "Kyle, which one should go first? What would you put second, Tina? What's next, Adam? Let's read it again. Does it make sense now?" Examples are provided below.

Example 1

4	Now Jan wears her helmet when she is on a bike.
3	She never forgot how much it hurt.
1	Last year Jan fell off her bike and hit her head.
2	She did not have a helmet on.

Example 2

4	Finally he got home.
2	Then he put things into his backpack.
1	First Sam cleaned off his desk.
3	After that Sam got on the bus.

Example 3

2	He bought a new VCR.
1	Mr. Keys went to the store.
4	He took it back the next week.
3	When he got home, the VCR did not work.

Strategies: Stairstep Sequencer

✤ Stairstep Sequencer

To use a stairstep graphic organizer, determine the climax and write it on the top step. Next, choose the two main events leading to the climax and put them on the left steps. Then, choose the two main events after the climax and write them on the right steps. Remind students who are retelling a historical event that they need to attend to dates, times, and sequence signal words.

The Pilgrims Came to America

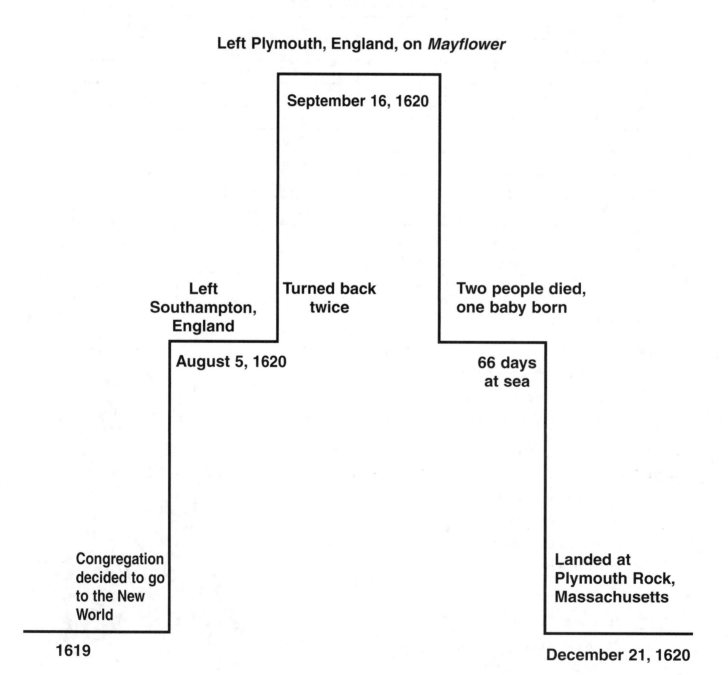

Left Plymouth, England, on *Mayflower*

September 16, 1620

Left Southampton, England

Turned back twice

Two people died, one baby born

August 5, 1620

66 days at sea

Congregation decided to go to the New World

Landed at Plymouth Rock, Massachusetts

1619

December 21, 1620

Strategies: Stairstep Sequencer *(cont.)*

Graphic Organizer

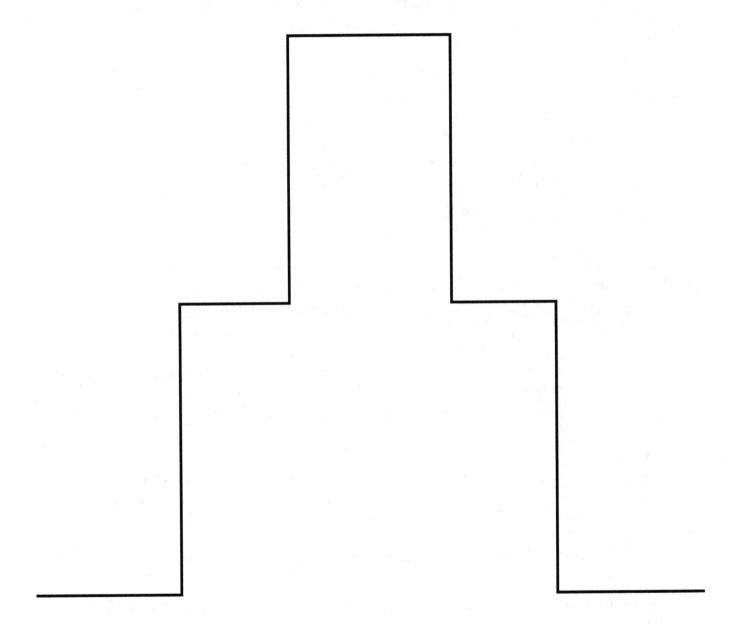

Strategies: Teaching Comparison; Comparison Chart

❖ Teaching Comparison

Comparison signal words compare or contrast two people, places, things, or ideas. To introduce the concept, write the example sentences below on the board or overhead. The signal words are italicized in each of the sentences. Have volunteers come up and underline the comparison signal words in each one. Give enough examples so that you have presented all of the signal words appropriate for your class's needs. Follow up by having the class read a passage and identify the signal words. Here are some examples:

Unless it stopped snowing, I could not go.

This pie is the *best*.

Tom did not mean to stare, *yet* he could not look away.

That hat is a *smaller* one.

Although Judy always got good marks, her brother Brian did not.

He wanted to leave, *but* he had to wait.

Shane could *either* eat the meat *or* be hungry.

❖ Comparison Chart

Many students enjoy listening to or reading the biography of a famous person, especially those that tell about the person's childhood. Use the biography of a historical figure to introduce comparison relationships using the chart on page 83. Fill in the life events column, then photocopy it and ask the students to fill in the other two columns. Here is an example:

Life Events of Harriett Tubman	Me, too	Explain
She tried to protect a slave from his master.	X	I stand up for other kids when bullies tease them.
She got a serious injury.		
She took care of a baby.	X	I watch my little brother a lot.
She prayed a lot.		
She worked in the fields.	X	I help my parents with our garden.
She helped others to be free.		

Is this person like you? If **yes**, circle the "is" and complete the sentence. If **no**, circle the "is not" and complete the sentence.

Harriet Tubman ((is), **is not**) like me because we both stood up for others. We have both taken care of little kids. We helped grow plants.

Strategies: Comparison Chart *(cont.)*

Graphic Organizer

Life Events of _____	Me, too	Explain

Is this person like you? If **yes**, circle "is" and complete the sentence. If **no**, circle "is not" and complete the sentence.

_____ (**is**, **is not**) like me because _____

_____

_____.

Strategies: The Handy 5Ws

❖ The Handy 5Ws

When you first introduce summarizing, you will need to give a lot of scaffolding before the students can sum up information independently. The basis of any summary are the five "handy" questions: who, what, when, where, and why. Using the Handy 5Ws graphic organizer on page 85 after reading a passage will give students a simple way to summarize a passage. Use a photocopier to make an overhead transparency of page 85. Present the first sentence and ask the students to tell you what information to put on each finger. Then erase the transparency and do the same for each sentence below. Point out how the answers to each question fall in different places in different sentences. Also, not every statement will have something on each finger.

Sentence 1: Columbus sailed across the Atlantic Ocean in 1492 in search of a new way to India.

Sentence 2: Cave people made drawings on cave walls to show about their lives.

Sentence 3: Long ago people walked across the Bering Land Bridge to look for a new home.

Sentence 4: During the 1960s Martin Luther King, Jr. worked to gain equality for all people.

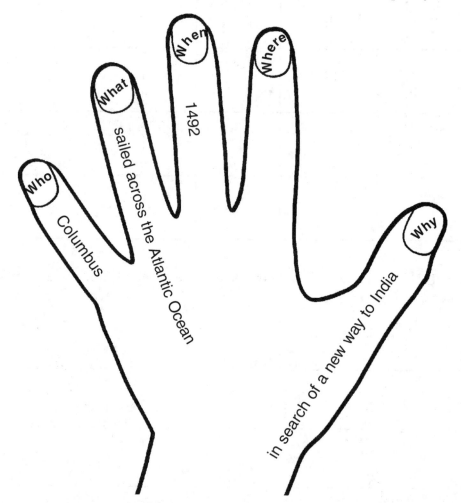

Select some sentences or paragraphs from nonfiction passages. Write each on a large sheet of butcher paper. For each sentence call on a different student to come up and fill in the chart. Once the students demonstrate understanding, pair them and ask the partners to complete the Handy 5Ws after reading a short expository selection.

Strategies: The Handy 5Ws *(cont.)*

Graphic Organizer

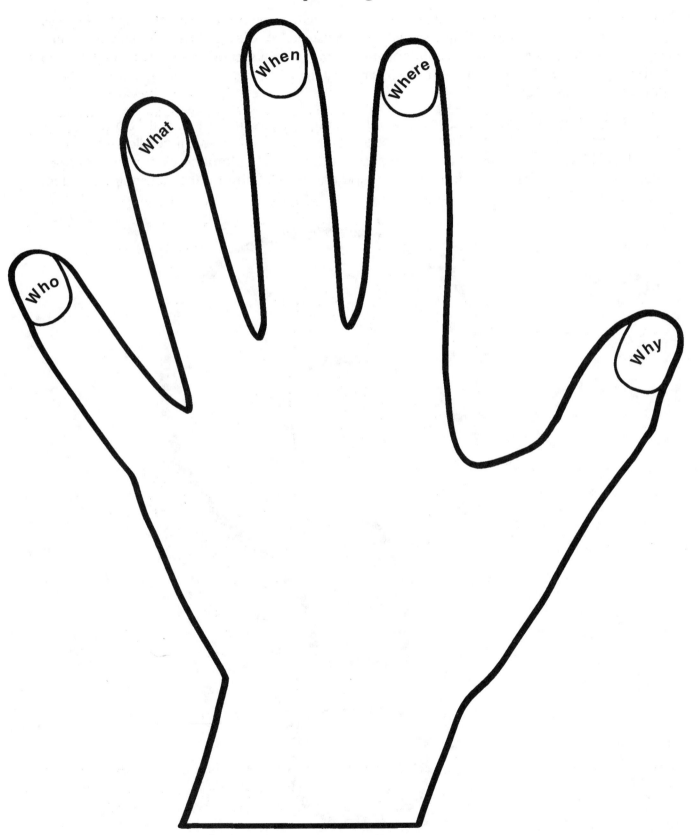

Strategies: Essential Questions

✥ Essential Questions

The Essential Questions graphic organizer on page 87 aids your students in pinpointing the key data in a passage. Use a photocopier to make an overhead transparency of page 87. After reading a nonfiction piece, ask the students to tell you what information to put in each section. Give your students additional practice by having them summarize passages the whole class has already read. The following is an example:

A deer is afraid when it is in an open field. Other animals might attack it. So the deer tears off big pieces of leaves and branches. But it does not chew. It swallows them whole! The food gets stored in a special part of the deer's stomach. When a deer feels safe, it brings up the stored food, or cud, and chews it. Chewing the cud helps the deer to digest its food.

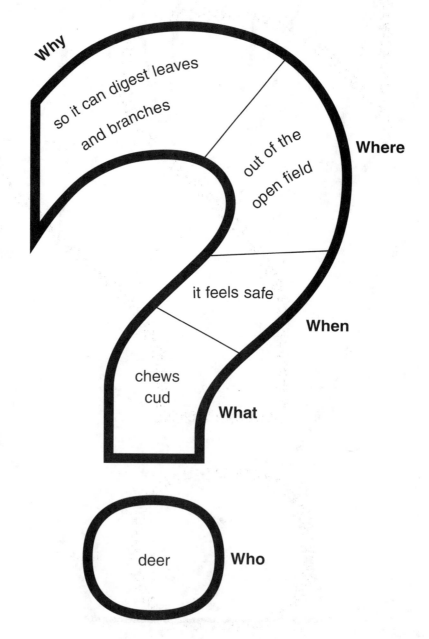

Strategies: Essential Questions *(cont.)*

Graphic Organizer

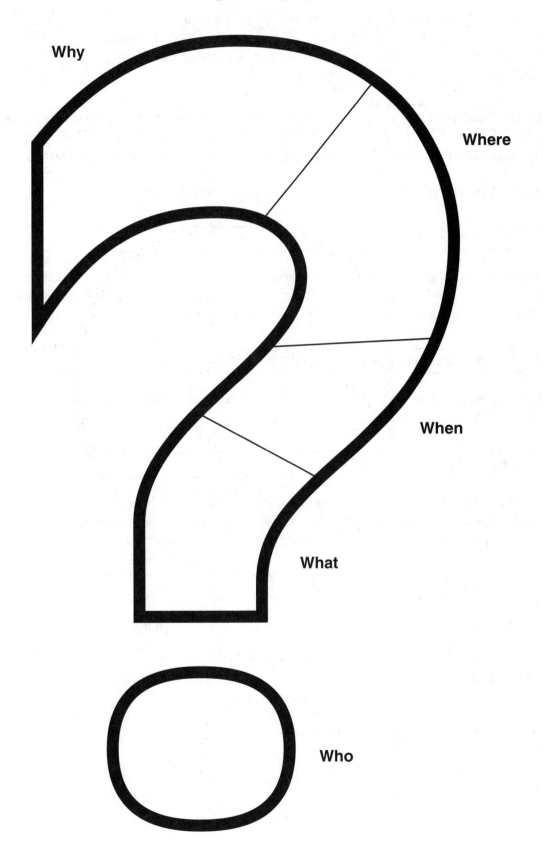

Strategies: Self-Monitored Reading

✛ Self-Monitoring Reading Strategy

Vaughen and Estes (1986) encourage readers to ask questions and independently find answers. Prominently display a poster stating the steps in this strategy. Direct the students to refer to the poster often. The strategy is best taught through several series of think-alouds in materials that you personally find challenging.

Step 1: Do I understand?

Read a paragraph. Then ask, "Do I really understand everything in this paragraph?"

Use a pencil to put a light X next to each paragraph you totally comprehend.

Step 2: What have I just read?

At the end of each paragraph, stop and summarize silently to yourself in your own words what you have read. You may look back at the text during this activity. Make a light pencil question mark next to each paragraph that contains anything that you do not understand

Step 3: Does it make sense now?

Finish reading the passage. Return to each paragraph that has a penciled question mark next to it and reread. Does it make sense now? If so, great! If not, move to step 4.

Step 4: Why am I having this trouble?

Pinpoint the trouble: Is the difficulty unfamiliar words or concepts? Is the sentence structure too complex? Is it because I know so little background information about the topic? Emphasize to students the importance of their figuring out their specific stumbling blocks before moving to step 5.

Step 5: Where can I get help?

Try a variety of aids: glossary, appendix, dictionary, chapter summary, etc. If self-help fails, ask a classmate or teacher for assistance.

As students become more comfortable with this strategy, make a rule that the students cannot ask for your help unless they can do both of the following:

◆ identify the exact source of their confusion

◆ describe the steps they've already taken on their own to resolve the problem.

Strategies: Bookmark

✣ Independent Reading Bookmark

When your students are ready to read independently, promote good reading habits by having them create and use bookmarks. Make a poster similar to the bookmark shown below (adapted from Blachowicz and Ogle, 2001). Display it in your classroom and refer to it often. Photocopy this page for each student. Cut out construction paper strips and let the students decorate one side in any way that they choose. They should write their names on that side, too. On the flip side, cut and paste the graphic below. For durability, laminate the bookmarks or cover them with clear Contact™ paper. Insist that students use their bookmarks and try these strategies before asking for assistance.

Before I read:

What do I already know?

- read title and headings

- look for words in different print

- look at pictures, graphs, and maps

What do I want to know?

As I read: **?????**

Do I understand?

- yes (keep reading)

- no (read over)

After I read:

Did I find answers to my questions?

- retell all I can recall

- I can remember by . . .

- I can find out more by . . .

What have I learned?

Introduction to Section 6: Writing Nonfiction

Writing is one of the most difficult skills to teach because it is a multifaceted, complex task, encompassing a broad range of abilities. Students may be asked to summarize a passage or to compose a response to a presentation they heard. They may need to take a stance and defend it. Like all writers, they must consider what to include, choose appropriate words, and sequence the material in a logical order. That's a tall order for anyone, let alone a child!

For a discussion on the developmental stages of spelling and writing, refer to the Emerging Reading and Writing Skills section (pages 57–62).

The Writing Process

Fortunately, no one has to write something perfectly on the first try. Students need to know that published authors—even the most famous ones—spend many hours rewriting, revising, and reorganizing. The steps in the writing process are as follows:

1. brainstorming/idea gathering—for ideas, see Preparing Students for Nonfiction (pages 13–28)
2. categorizing and clustering ideas—for ideas, see Preparing Students for Nonfiction
3. writing a first draft
4. conferencing with a teacher or peer
5. revising for clarity, possibly reorganizing
6. writing a second draft
7. revising for accurate spelling, grammar, punctuation, etc.
8. publishing and sharing the final copy with others

All formal writing should follow the steps of the writing process. However, with informal writing, such as learning logs or graphic organizers, students should get their ideas down without regard for spelling, grammar, or mechanics.

Strategies: Learning Logs

✛ Learning Logs

Learning logs encourage students to share their ideas and questions in a safe environment. A student who rarely speaks in class may write volumes in a journal. Reading and responding to a student's journal is like having a private conversation with that student. Having students keep learning logs will provide individual feedback for both of you.

You can use learning logs in different ways. Have students summarize what they have learned and what they still don't understand after a lesson. Tell students to ask questions they'd like answered. Students can also write their questions and record the answers as they discover them, submitting the journal to you only when a question remains unanswered near the end of a unit. Some primary grade teachers have students write the highlights from the weekend each Monday morning. Whatever method you select, journal writing works best when done for about 10 minutes daily, especially if you participate by writing in your own journal at the same time.

Strategies: Active Verbs; Reluctant Writers

✛ Using Nouns and Active Verbs

Students' writing will improve through the use of nouns and active verbs. Encourage this with the following exercise:

Choose a familiar topic (in this example, *the forest*). Have the class brainstorm a list of related nouns. Have the class brainstorm a list of actions (verbs) that each noun could do. Ask the students to write a paragraph using the nouns and verbs.

Nouns (people, places, things, ideas)	**Verbs** (what each noun can do)
tree	stands, sways
sunlight	shines, glows, hides
bees	buzz, hum, fly
birds	fly, sing, chirp
branches	bend, break, rattle
rabbit	hops, runs, eats, twitches nose

Here's a student's composition based on the words generated. The words from the brainstorm lists are in bold print:

On this warm summer day, **sunlight shines** through the **trees** of the forest. The air is filled with the sound of **bees buzzing**. **Birds chirp** as they **fly** from **branch to branch**. A **rabbit hops** by.

✛ Helping Reluctant Writers

Give immediate assistance to any reluctant writers to keep frustration to a minimum. Encourage students to always prepare an illustration prior to writing. This not only helps them to collect their thoughts, it combats writer's block. When a child feels overwhelmed by a blank sheet of paper, say, "What do you want to say about your picture?"

After a student has drawn a picture, you can say, "Tell me about your picture." Listen to his or her response and then ask, "If you had written words to accompany your picture, where would they go?" Once the child indicates where the writing would go, offer to do the writing by asking, "Would you like me to write something there? What should I write?"

Primary grade children often feel frustrated because ideas come to them faster than they can get them on paper. Because it is so challenging for children to think of what they want to say, how they want to say it, and to write at the same time, have your students record their ideas onto a tape recorder. Later they can transcribe the tape, rewinding as many times as necessary. Once it's transcribed, the student can revise and edit to improve the mechanics of his or her message.

In addition, using magnet words enable children to bypass the often grueling small motor task of forming letters and erasing while composing and editing. Large bookstores and educational supply catalogs offer packages of magnetic words.

Strategies: Pattern Writing; Personal Events

✣ Pattern Writing

Get your students to write nonfiction without even knowing it by having them write following a familiar pattern. Suppose a student was writing about the types of animals found in a zoo. Prepare a paragraph frame that follows "Old McDonald" and have him or her fill it in. For example:

Old McDonald had <u>a zoo</u>. E-I-E-I-O

And in this zoo he had <u>a lion</u>. E-I-E-I-O

With a <u>roar, roar</u> here and a <u>roar roar</u> there,

Here a <u>roar</u>, there a <u>roar</u>, everywhere a <u>roar roar</u>!

Old McDonald had <u>a zoo</u>. E-I-E-I-O

And in this zoo he had <u>a monkey</u>. E-I-E-I-O

With a <u>chee chee</u> here and a <u>chee chee</u> there

Here a <u>chee</u>, there a <u>chee</u>, everywhere a <u>chee chee</u>!

Other good patterns include Laura Joffe Numeroff's *If You Give a Pig a Pancake* (HarperCollins, 1998) and Margaret Wise Brown's *The Important Book* (HarperCollins, 1999). Students can follow the format of *The Important Book* when writing. For example:

The important thing about subtraction is that you always get a smaller number than you started with.

Sometimes subtraction is called "take away" or "finding the difference."

You use a minus sign to show subtraction.

But the important thing about subtraction is that you always get a smaller number than you started with.

✣ Writing About Personal Events

Tell the students that they are famous and a journalist wants to report to the public how they spend their leisure time. Ask them to compose a paragraph or two about their weekend by recording in their journals all the events of the past weekend in the order in which they occurred. Note: If you have some "couch potatoes," have them write which shows they watched or video games they played and describe what happened in them.

Strategies: Past Events; Experience Writing; Nonfiction Books

✛ Writing About a Past Event

Historians must use a variety of resources to determine what happened in the past. Demonstrate this by asking your students to write everything they remember about their most recent birthdays. They may be surprised by how little they recall. Encourage them to find out more (referring to photographs or a home videotape; asking parents, siblings, and friends) in order to reconstruct that date. After conducting their investigation, have them add to their composition the extra information they gained.

✛ Experience Writing

Experience writing shows students how to put together a composition about a personally experienced event. Consider the needs of your class to determine how many sessions this will take.

1. Take a field trip.

2. As a whole group, brainstorm all that you recall from the trip. Record the information.

3. Ask the students to sort the information into three categories.

4. Using an overhead, guide the students in using as many words in each group as possible to compose three paragraphs (one for each category). Write each paragraph on its own transparency.

5. Have the class suggest different sequences for the paragraphs on the overhead. Demonstrate this by rearranging the individual transparencies. After each organization, have the class chorally read the piece from start to finish.

6. The class votes to determine the order of the paragraphs.

7. Ask for beginning sentence suggestions. Record these on another transparency. Read them aloud to the class and have the class vote on the best beginning.

8. Ask for concluding sentence suggestions. Record these on another transparency. Read them aloud to the class and have the class vote on the best conclusion.

9. Prepare a final version with the paragraph organization and opening and closing sentences the students selected. Photocopy it and hand it out to each class member.

10. Have the students copy this into their journals or draw illustrations to accompany it.

✛ Creating Nonfiction Books

Fold two sheets of paper in half and staple them inside a folded piece of a construction paper to make a simple, eight-page book for each student. Ask students to list two or three topics (soccer, judo, horses) they know a lot about. Have the students choose which topic they are most expert in and ask themselves, "What do my readers need to know to understand (topic)?" Each child will share his or her personal knowledge by designing a nonfiction book, complete with a title page and illustrations. Encourage them to include appropriate text treatments they have seen in published informational texts (such as headings, underlining, captions, etc.). In addition to building self-esteem with this project, you may be amazed at what you learn from your young "experts."

Strategies: Family Members; Posters

✛ Writing About Family Members

Students can act as detectives assigned to a specific family member for two days without the person realizing it. Instruct them to not invade the person's privacy (by looking inside a purse, pockets, drawers, etc.). Ask the students to jot down facts about the person so that they can prepare a paragraph. Show an example when you first give the assignment and keep it posted until everyone is finished composing. Here's a well-written factual paragraph that a second grader wrote about his teenage brother:

> Nate gets up late and misses the bus. So he has to walk to school. He wears big loose jeans and T-shirts. He talks on the phone a lot and won't let anyone come in his room. Nate does his homework late at night.

✛ Nonfiction Book Report Poster

Ask parents to read a nonfiction picture book on a topic of interest to their child. If the child is proficient enough, he or she may choose to read the book independently.

Have the students create a poster advertising the book. The poster should include the book's title, the author's name, at least five important facts, and at least three colored illustrations with captions. On the back of the poster the child dictates or writes three or more sentences about what he or she most likes about the book. When the child is finished, he or she evaluates his or her own poster by filling out the graphic organizer on page 95.

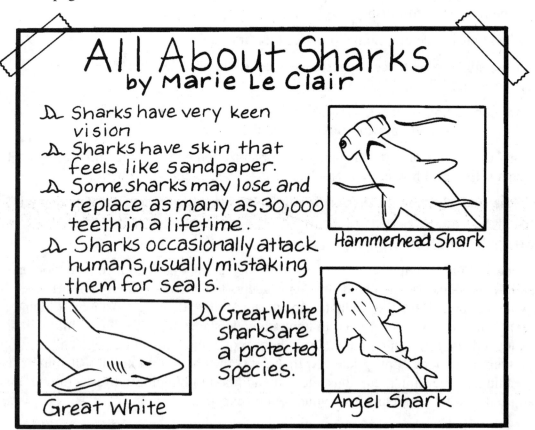

Strategies: Posters *(cont.)*

Dear Parent,

Your child is going to do a nonfiction book poster. Please help your child select a nonfiction picture book and read it aloud to him or her by _____ . If your child selects a book that he or she is capable of reading, let the child read it. Use the five-finger test to see if book qualifies for independent reading. Have the child open to a page in the center of the book and hold up a finger every time he or she comes to an unfamiliar word. If the child raises five or more fingers, the book is too difficult and must be read to the child.

Your child will create a poster advertising the book. The poster should include:

✦ the book's title

✦ the author's name

✦ at least five important facts

✦ at least three colored illustrations with captions

On the back of the poster the child writes (or dictates to you) three or more sentences about what he or she likes most about the book.

When your child is done, have him or her assess the poster using the evaluation form below. This form must be submitted with the poster.

- -

Rate-Your-Book Poster

Name _____ Due _____

Book Title _____

Author _____

Look at your poster. Put the checkmark (✔) in a column that answers each question.

Yes	Sort of	No	
			Content: The poster has the author's name, book title, and at least five facts and three colored pictures with captions.
			Appearance: Pictures are big and cover most of the space. Drawings are colored. Print is neat and big enough. Mistakes are neatly corrected.
			Spelling: The author's name, book title, and picture captions are spelled correctly.
			Paragraph: The back of the poster has three or more sentences about the best part of the book.

Strategies: Triangle Poetry

Triangle Poetry Organizer

The triangle graphic organizer on page 97 has students demonstrate the highlights of what they have learned through nonfiction poetry:

- ✦ 1 word for subject
- ✦ 2 describing words
- ✦ 3 words that tell what it does
- ✦ 4 word phrase that tells something about it
- ✦ synonym (if possible) *or* name subject again

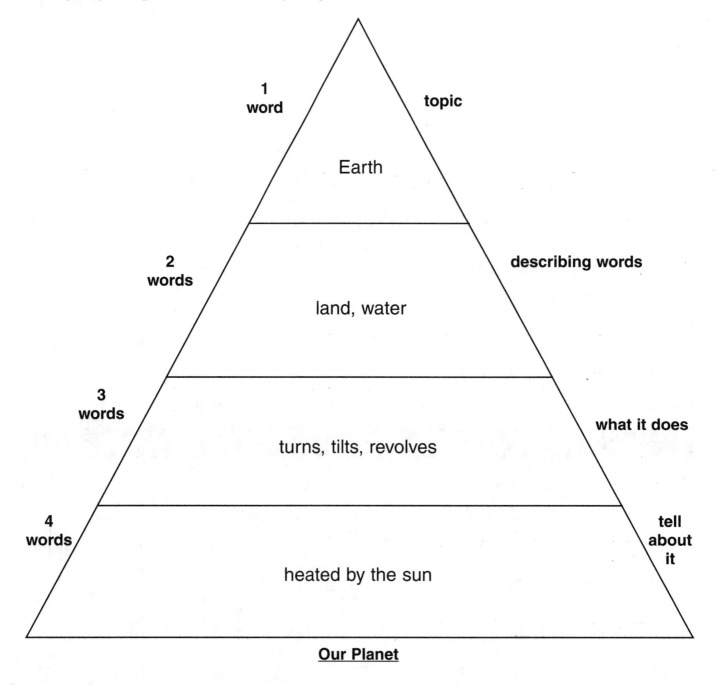

1 word   **topic**

Earth

2 words   **describing words**

land, water

3 words   **what it does**

turns, tilts, revolves

4 words   **tell about it**

heated by the sun

Our Planet

Strategies: Triangle Poetry *(cont.)*

Graphic Organizer

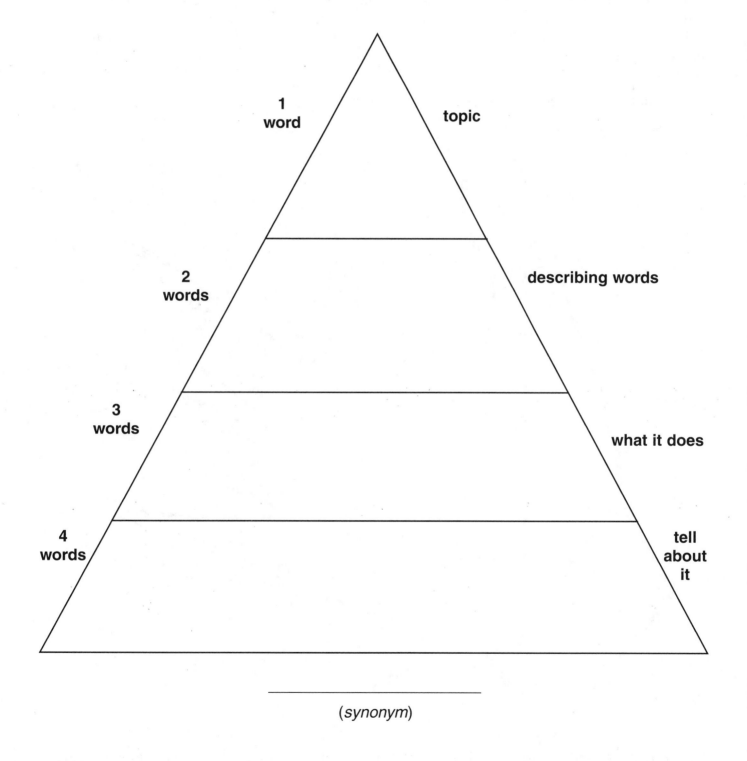

1
word   topic

2
words   describing words

3
words   what it does

4
words   tell
                        about
                        it

_____

(synonym)

Strategies: Five-Sentence Paragraph

✛ Five-Sentence Paragraph

When students are learning to write independent paragraphs, they need a great deal of structure. Give students the topic, opening, and closing sentences. Teach them to think of one sentence to write on each of the fingers of the graphic organizer on page 99. Then have them arrange the five sentences to form a paragraph on the back of the paper. Do this as a whole class several times before letting the students try it independently.

Opening: A balanced diet is important. Eat different foods.

Closing: They are not good for you.

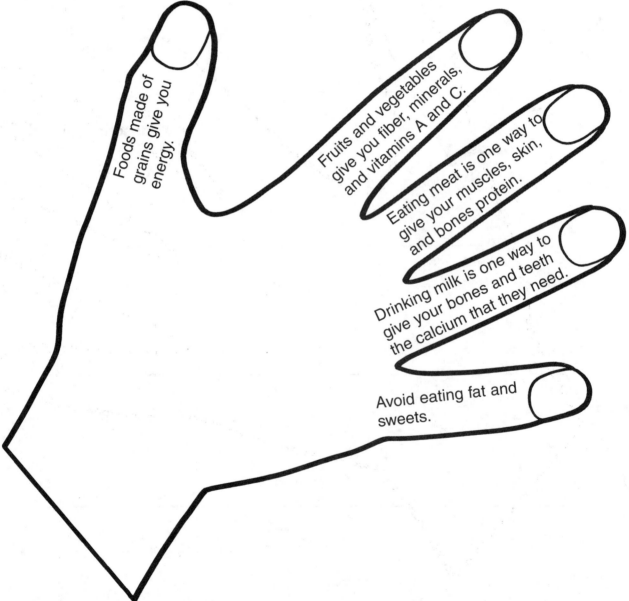

Foods made of grains give you energy.

Fruits and vegetables give you fiber, minerals, and vitamins A and C.

Eating meat is one way to give your muscles, skin, and bones protein.

Drinking milk is one way to give your bones and teeth the calcium that they need.

Avoid eating fat and sweets.

Resulting paragraph: A balanced diet is important. Eat different foods. Foods made of grains give you energy. Fruits and vegetables give you fiber, minerals, and vitamins A and C. Eating meat is one way to give your muscles, skin, and bones protein. Drinking milk is one way to give your bones and teeth the calcium that they need. Avoid eating fat and sweets. They are not good for you.

Strategies: Five-Sentence Paragraph (cont.)

Graphic Organizer

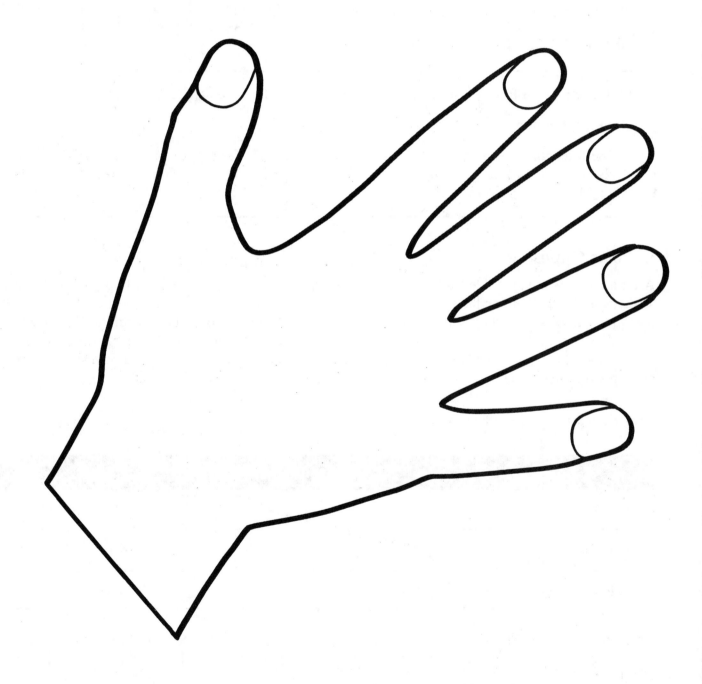

Strategies: Paragraph Frame; Polar Opposites

✛ Paragraph Frame

After students have learned how to fill in sentence frames and participated in sentence building exercises, they can write three- or four-sentence paragraphs using a frame. Prepare a frame by asking a question immediately followed by a paragraph with ideas stated in logical, sequential order but with key information missing. Students copy the entire paragraph, filling in the blanks. Explain to students that the blanks do not necessarily stand for just one word. A paragraph frame is given out after listening or reading. Here's an example:

> **Question:** What force causes things to fall to the ground? Who named this force?
>
> **Paragraph Frame:**
>
> The force that makes things fall to the ground is <u>gravity</u>. <u>Gravity</u> keeps us on the ground. It also keeps the Moon going <u>around the Earth</u>. <u>Sir Isaac Newton</u> named this force after <u>watching an apple fall from a tree</u>.

✛ Polar Opposites

After a unit of study, provide students with a Polar Opposites scale (Bean and Bishop, 1992). Have the students indicate where on the scale they believe each concept falls. From the chart below, you can tell the student knows that Alaska has few people and is almost always cold. The student also demonstrates the understanding that Alaska is neither dark nor bright because it spends half of each year as each. After students have completed the polar opposites scale, they can write or dictate a paragraph using the concepts from the scale.

Directions: Put an X in the box closest to what is true.

Alaska				
few people	X			many people
hot			X	cold
bright		X		dark

Few people live in Alaska. Alaska is cold most of the time. The state is dark for about six months each year. The sun hardly rises. Then it has six months of daylight. It stays bright all night.

Strategies: RAFT

❖ Creative Nonfiction Writing: RAFT

Students can respond to expository text in a wide variety of ways. RAFT (Santa, 1988) is an acronym for Role, Audience, Form, and Topic. The students put themselves into a specified role, consider their audience and its needs, and craft a certain kind of document about the assigned topic. This challenges students to actively process in order to prepare a unique creative response.

Since this is a new and different way for students to demonstrate their knowledge, always provide an example prior to assigning students a specific RAFT project. You can prepare the example or show one that student did in a past class. Post these three questions that the students must answer in order to do the assignment:

- ✦ What do I think about this?

- ✦ Who am I telling?

- ✦ What should I say?

Have them show you the answers to their questions before they attempt to compose the piece.

The following chart suggests some of the nonfiction pieces that you could have your students compose. Each suggestion is followed by an example.

Your Role	Audience for piece	Form	Topic
travel agent	tourists	pamphlet	reasons to visit your state
Johnny Appleseed	self	diary	planting trees across America
nurse	patients	Web page	how to treat a minor cut
veterinarian	cat owners	manual	how to take care of a cat
ad copy writer	anyone	advertisement	elements of a well-balanced diet
editor	magazine readers	FAQ	all about sound
chef	other cooks and chefs	instructions	assembling a favorite sandwich
children's author	preschooler	picture book	desert animals
graphic designer	science-fair audience	poster	life cycle of a frog
historical figure	friends	scrapbook	memorabilia of lifetime
new writer	public	newspaper article	discovery of Pluto
Ann Landers	early colonists	advice column	how to survive in the New World
metal can	public	thank you note	glad it was recycled
literary expert	other students in your grade	book review	why they should read a certain nonfiction book
self	own parents	e-mail message	request for school supplies replenishment
spider pet owner	people who dislike spiders	poem	persuade them that spiders are good

Strategies: Learning to Summarize; Television Show Summary; 3-2-1 Summary

❖ Learning to Summarize: Today's Story

At the end of each day, ask the students to help you to summarize the day. As they talk, type the story into a word-processing program. Include two signature lines at the bottom, print it out, and make copies. Send a copy home with each child. The students read the day's summary to their parents that night. The parent and student both sign the summary and return it to class the next day. Do this on four consecutive days to solidify the concept of summary:

Today's Story

[Your name] took attendance and lunch count. We said the Pledge of Allegiance. Then we made chalk drawings in art. Next, we learned some new vocabulary words and read *Time for Kids* magazine. Then it was snack time. After that we did subtraction problems. . . . [etc.]

❖ Television Show Summary

Have the students write a two- or three-sentence summary of a television show the class watched. For example, after watching a Bill Nye video on the water cycle, your class could create this summary of the show:

Every bit of Earth's water is always in some part of the water cycle. The cycle is evaporation, condensation, precipitation, and storage (lakes, icebergs). Water never leaves the system, and no new water enters the system.

❖ 3-2-1 Summary

After learning about a subject, students are asked to write a 3-2-1 summary based on this format:

3 = things that really interest you; important events in person's life; important characteristics of a plant or animal

2 = things you'd like to find out more about; questions you'd like to ask the author; questions about the topic; ways plant or animal is useful

1 = new fact you learned

Strategies: Monthly Recap

❖ Monthly Recap

Show students how to summarize by doing a monthly recap. Post a large calendar. Each day, record a word or phrase that the class feels will let them recall that particular day. At the end of the month, create a small version of the calendar (page 104) and photocopy it. Then students take the calendar home and prepare a summary of the month by writing about three most memorable activities from each week. First graders dictate their summaries to a parent. Second graders fill in a paragraph frame (page 105). Third graders can complete the paragraph frame for a rough draft, then write a final copy, using proper paragraph form. The following is an example of a class's calendar and the resulting monthly recap:

October

Monday	Tuesday	Wednesday	Thursday	Friday
		1 DARE assembly	2 played Red Rover in gym	3 Quiz on addition facts
6 Listened to: <u>The Bus Driver from the Black Lagoon</u>	7 Played dodgeball in gym	8 Went to Mr. Weaver's class play	9 Used Skittles to practice subtraction facts	10 Red Ribbon day
13 No school: Columbus Day	14 The zoomobile came	15 Field trip to pumpkin farm	16 Wrote experience story about pumpkin farm	17 African storyteller told the story of "Mufaro's Beautiful Daughters"
20 Fire prevention week—made escape plans for own home	21 Open house	22 Firefighters showed us their truck, and we crawled through a smoke tunnel.	23 Quiz on subtraction facts	24 Made baking soda volcanoes in science
27 Everyone passed Friday's spelling test! 45 minutes of playground time!	28 Listened to <u>Alexander and the Terrible, Horrible, No Good, Very Bad Day</u>	29 Sang "Ten Little Pumpkins" in music class	30 Finished making world globes in art class	31 Harvest party with cider and popcorn balls

Monthly Recap for <u>October</u>

In the first week of <u>October</u>, we <u>went to the DARE assembly, played Red Rover, and had a quiz on addition facts</u>. The next week, we <u>played dodgeball, went to Mr. Weaver's class play, and used Skittles to do math</u>.

Then <u>the zoomobile came. We went on a field trip to the pumpkin farm and listened to an African storyteller. For fire-prevention week we made home escape plans and got to see a fire truck and crawl through a smoke tunnel.</u> During the last week of <u>October</u>, we <u>had a harvest party, sang "Ten Little Pumpkins," and got 45 extra minutes of playground time</u>.

Strategies: Monthly Recap *(cont.)*

_____

(month)

Monday	Tuesday	Wednesday	Thursday	Friday

Strategies: Monthly Recap *(cont.)*

Monthly Recap for _____

In the first week of _____ , we

_____

_____

_____

_____

The next week,

_____

_____

_____

_____

Then

_____

_____

_____

_____

During the last week of _____ , we

_____

_____

_____

_____

Strategies: Cause-Effect Relationships

✥ Writing About Cause-Effect Relationships

Schmidt and Buckley (1991) designed a chart to help young students understand fictional plots. This adaptation of their idea will let you teach your students to concisely summarize what they have learned during a unit of study. Make a transparency of the blank graphic organizer on page 107. Then discuss a historical event with a clear cause-and-effect relationship (the example below tells the story of the Statue of Liberty.) Have the students prompt you to fill in the graphic organizer on the overhead. Show them how to compose a three-sentence summary of the cause-and-effect relationship. If you compile the paragraphs they become a short essay.

Cause and Effect Chart

Someone or Something	Wanted	But	So
people of France	to give America a birthday gift	the statue of liberty was huge	they put it in 214 boxes on a ship
The people of France wanted to give America the Statue of Liberty as a birthday gift. But it was too big to send all in one piece. So they packed it in 214 boxes and sent it on a ship.			
The statue	needed a base	there was no money to build one	a NY newspaper said it would print the name of those who gave any money to build the base
The statue needed a base, but there was no money to build one. So a New York newspaper printed the name of every person who gave money to build the base. Finally, enough money was raised for the base.			

Strategies: Cause-Effect Relationships *(cont.)*

Graphic Organizer

Someone or Something	Wanted	But	So

Strategies: Magnet Summaries

✥ Magnet Summaries

With this variation of Magnet Summaries (Buehl, 2001), students identify facts related to key terms (magnet words) in a text. They record the magnet word and related facts onto a magnet and use them to write a concise summary on the bar of steel.

1. Introduce the technique by demonstrating the interaction of a magnet and steel. Explain that just as magnets are drawn to steel, magnet words draw facts to them.

2. Choose a magnet term or phrase. Select magnet terms to which many facts can be applied. In this example, the magnet term is "American Immigration."

3. Using a photocopier make an overhead transparency of the graphic organizer on page 109. Distribute copies of the page to the students, too. Display the transparency showing the first magnet word you've chosen. Have students write it between the prongs of the magnet. Then ask students to recall important details that relate to that magnet word. They can refer to the passage.

4. Have students offer examples of words or phrases they want to write on the prongs of the magnet. Write these on your overhead magnet as they do the same on theirs.

5. When you have written about four details for the magnet word, ask the class to generate a brief summary on the bar of steel using all the words on the magnet.

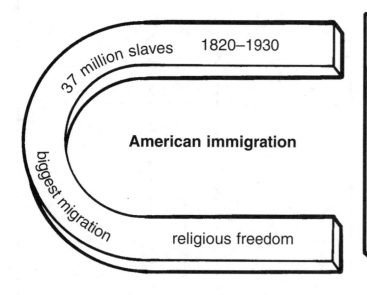

American immigration

37 million slaves   1820–1930

biggest migration

religious freedom

Between 1820–1930, 37 million people came to the United States from Europe and Africa. It was the biggest movement of people ever. The Africans came as slaves. The Europeans came to seek a better life and have religious freedom.

Strategies: Magnet Summaries (cont.)

Graphic Organizer

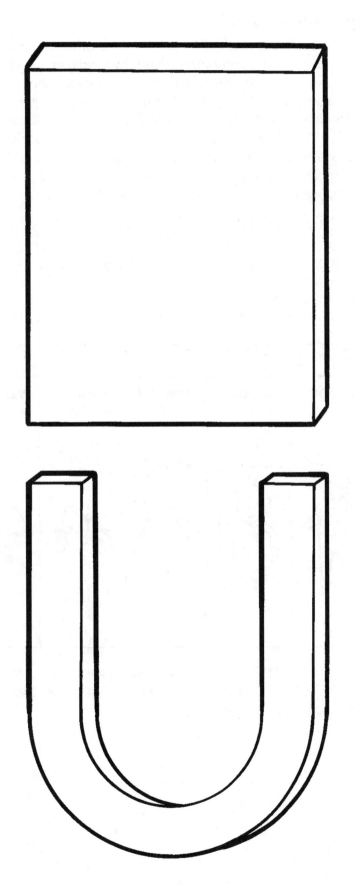

Strategies: Autobiography

✥ Preparing an Autobiography

Students will understand the concept of biography better after creating their own autobiography. Copy page 111 and send it home. If a parent fails to return the paper, ask the child to guess when each event occurred. Create time lines by cutting a strip of butcher paper about 24" long and 4" wide for each child. Write these ages across the top in even intervals: for first grade, use 0–7; for second grade use 0–8, and for third grade use 0–9. Distribute the time lines and tell the children that they will be creating a time line of important events in their lives. Explain that the numbers stand for their ages (0 being their birth). Have the children cut out the pictures from page 111 and paste them under the correct number. Emphasize that everyone will not have the same pictures or even the same number of pictures. Ask the students who finish quickly to color the pictures on their time lines.

Depending on your students' abilities, have them dictate or write an autobiography based on their time lines. Each time line will be unique. In the following example you can see that this first grader has not yet learned to swim or pump a swing. She also has not had any new babies born into her family.

0	1	2	3	4	5	5 1/2	6
born	walked	talked	dressed self	rode a bike	went to school	tied shoes	lost first tooth

I was born on August 5, 1999. I learned to walk when I was one. By two, I could talk. At three, I dressed myself. At four, I rode a bike. When I was five, I went to school and I tied my shoes. I lost my first tooth at age six.

Strategies: Autobiography *(cont.)*

Parent Letter

Dear Parents:

We are creating autobiographies as an introduction to biographies. Please look at the pictures below and tell your child the age at which he or she did each one. Do only the pictures that have already happened in your child's life. Have your child write the age in the box in the corner by each picture. Ages must be in whole or half years (for example, 2 years, 2 ½ years, etc.). Your child will use these pictures to create a time line of these milestones. Your child will then use the time line to dictate or write an autobiography. Please return this page tomorrow. Thank you!

swam	dressed self	born
walked	talked	rode a bike
went to school	lost first tooth	tied shoes
held a baby	read a book alone	pumped a swing

Strategies: Biography

⁜ Preparing a Biography

After doing their autobiography, students may enjoy learning about historical figures. Some may choose to research and write a biography for an inquiry project (for more on inquiry projects, see Researching Nonfiction section). The youngest students can fill in the graphic organizer on page 113, write the names of the sources used on the back, and submit it as the final product. Older students can take notes on the graphic organizer, put bibliographic entries on the back of the figure, and use the information they record on it to write a more detailed report.

If you make extra copies of the page, students can decorate the figure to look like the person (by drawing or making construction-paper period clothes and hair for the figure). Then they cut out the decorated version, place it over the note-filled figure, and carefully staple it at the top.

You can also have students write biopoems (page 114) inside of this graphic organizer.

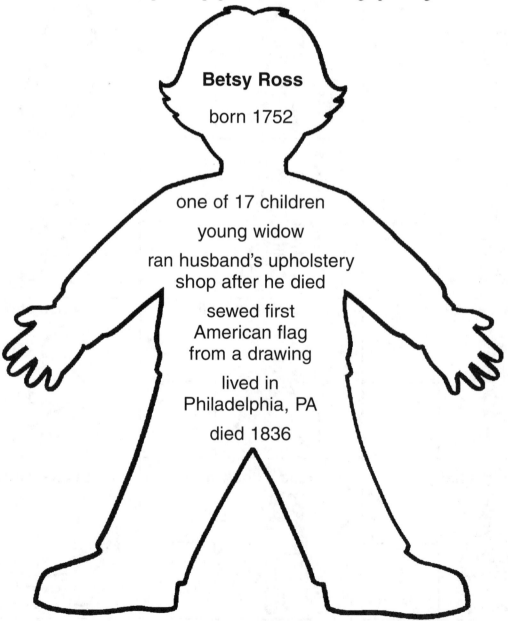

Betsy Ross

born 1752

one of 17 children

young widow

ran husband's upholstery
shop after he died

sewed first
American flag
from a drawing

lived in
Philadelphia, PA

died 1836

Strategies: Biography *(cont.)*

Graphic Organizer

Strategies: Biopoems; Summary Frame

⁜ Biopoems

Students can demonstrate their knowledge of famous people through biopoems (Gere, 1985):

Line 1—Person's first name

Line 2—Four character traits

Line 3—Relative of (wife, husband, daughter, son, mother, father, sister, brother)

Line 4—Lover of (list three people or things to which the person is devoted)

Line 5—Who feels/felt (list three emotions)

Line 6—Who needs/needed (list three items)

Line 7—Who fears/feared (list three items)

Line 8—Who wants/wanted (list three items)

Line 9—Resident of (can be birthplace, where resided at time of death, etc.)

Line 10—Person's last name

> George
>
> Intelligent, heroic, honest, brave
>
> Husband of Martha
>
> Lover of his home, his country, and freedom
>
> Who felt humble, determined, and courageous
>
> Who needed more supplies, trained soldiers, and battle plans
>
> Who feared not being able to take care of his men, a long war, and a British victory
>
> Who wanted freedom from Britain, an end to the Revolutionary War, and a strong nation
>
> Resident of Mount Vernon
>
> Washington

⁜ Summary Frame

Before reading a nonfiction passage, give students copies of the summary frame on page 115. Have the students write their individual responses after the "know" statement. Next, have the students read the material and complete the frame. The following is an example:

Before I started reading about <u>dolphins</u>, I knew <u>that they were sea animals. I had seen them do tricks at a show</u>.

In the article, I learned <u>dolphins are mammals. They are very smart. They live in pods and talk to each other with sounds</u>.

I also learned <u>that dolphins have saved people from drowning in the ocean</u>.

I was surprised <u>that dolphins are really small whales</u>.

Strategies: Summary Frame *(cont.)*

Graphic Organizer

Before I started reading about _____ , I knew

_____

_____

_____

_____

In the article, I learned

_____

_____

_____

I also learned

_____

_____

_____

I was surprised

_____

_____

_____

Strategies: Self-Editing; Editing Conferences; Peer Editing

✣ Self-Editing

In order for your students to excel at editing their own work, they must read their pieces aloud. This lets them hear if the writing is confusing. As they read, they should underline or circle the parts that seem rough and need fixing. Before submitting a final draft, students should look critically at their pieces, using the self-editing checklist on page 117. If students have any check marks in the "No" column, they must fix the problem.

✣ Editing Conferences

At editing conferences with students, your goal is to help the students to assess their own work. To do so, you must ask questions more often than you give suggestions. Here are some good questions to ask to make students reflect on the quality of their own work:

- ✦ What's the most important point? Why?

- ✦ Is there anything that doesn't seem to fit?

- ✦ Read aloud the best part. Why is this section better than the others?

- ✦ After reading this, I want to know _____. Could you answer it in your paper?

✣ Peer Editing

For peer-editing conferences, establish heterogeneous small groups. The first student writer reads his or her piece and asks for specific feedback, such as "Have I explained [the topic] clearly enough?" or "Can you think of a better way to say [what I have said]?" Group members give their suggestions for improvement. Then the next student writer presents his or her piece. They continue in this manner until all group members have had an opportunity to have their pieces critiqued.

Strategies: Self-Editing *(cont.)*

Graphic Organizers

Question	Yes	No
Is the writing easy to read?		
Are any words missing?		
Are there any extra words?		
Do all of the sentences begin with a capital?		
Do all of the sentences end with a punctuation mark?		
Are all of the words spelled correctly?		
Are the names of people and places capitalized?		

Do you have marks in the "No" column? If you do, go back and fix you work.

- -

Question	Yes	No
Is the writing easy to read?		
Are any words missing?		
Are there any extra words?		
Do all of the sentences begin with a capital?		
Do all of the sentences end with a punctuation mark?		
Are all of the words spelled correctly?		
Are the names of people and places capitalized?		

Do you have marks in the "No" column? If you do, go back and fix you work.

Strategies: Praise-Question-Polish

✤ Praise-Question-Polish

Praise-Question-Polish (Lyons, 1981) is a good way for peers to edit each other's work. Prominently post the steps of the strategy. After students have written a first draft, they meet with a partner. The first student reads his or her paper aloud, then asks:

Praise: "What do you like best?"

Question: "What questions do you have?"

Polish: "What kinds of additions or corrections are needed? Do I need to reorganize?"

These questions are repeated after the second partner reads his or her work aloud.

You can choose to have the students read each other's work and respond to it in writing by providing copies of the Praise-Question-Polish form on page 119.

Praise-Question-Polish

Trisha Bennett	Ahamed Alkaeer
(writer's name)	*(editor's name)*

Praise:

The part I like best is <u>how strong a snapping turtle's jaws are.</u>

Question:

I do not understand <u>how snapping turtles grow up after they hatch.</u>

Polish:

Maybe you should add <u>which animals eat snapping turtles.</u>

Maybe you should get rid of <u>the list of all the animals snapping turtles will eat. Just tell the most common ones.</u>

Strategies: Praise-Question-Polish

Graphic Organizer

_____   _____
           (writer's name)   *(editor's name)*

Praise:

The part I like best is _____

_____

_____

_____

Question:

I do not understand _____

_____

_____

Polish:

Maybe you should add_____

_____

_____

Maybe you should get rid of _____

_____

_____

Introduction to Section 7: Researching Nonfiction

Research always begins with a question. Suppose that you were considering having corrective laser surgery on your eyes. For your primary research, you would talk to ophthalmologists and other people who have had the procedure done. You might even visit a clinic to watch the procedure being done. For your secondary research, you might conduct Internet research and read pamphlets and magazine articles.

In pursuit of a genuine question of personal interest, you learned a great deal. In the same way, your students will be interested in doing research if you allow them to pursue their own questions, search to find the answers, and ultimately share their findings with others. Your students will learn the same research skills with less resistance by pursuing topics of their choice. It can also make a crucial difference in both the attitude and effort of the students who struggle or feel disenfranchised. If your district insists that students prepare a research project on a specific subject, try to define that topic as broadly as possible. For example, you can have your students pursue topics of their choice under a broad curricular area such as inventions or the Pacific Ocean.

Third grade is the earliest that students can be expected to independently prepare a research project. However, you should take your students as a whole class through the research process in the earlier grades. This section is written as though the entire class is pursuing the same research topic and questions; however, all of the information and strategies apply to third graders conducting independent research. Specific instructions for independent researchers are indicated where necessary.

Strategies: Inquiry-Based Research

✛ Inquiry-Based Research

These are the steps in inquiry-based research (Harvey, 1998):

1. Select a topic.

2. Come up with two meaningful questions about it. Think of a theory to answer each question.

3. Gather information from a variety of secondary sources (books, magazine articles, computer resources, videos, the Internet, etc.), preferably complemented by at least one primary source (interviews, field trips, museum displays, surveys, correspondence with experts, etc.).

4. Organize, interpret, and draw conclusions about the information obtained.

5. Share these conclusions with others.

Strategies: Selection of Topic; Helping Students

❖ Selection of Topic

Share inquiry projects from former classes. Expose students to a wide variety of topics by reading aloud from nonfiction trade books, newspapers, magazines, and Web sites. You can even share articles from adult nonfiction books or magazines that have spectacular photos (such as *National Geographic*).

Let students choose materials to look at and read in order to find topics that interest them. Provide nonfiction books and magazines below grade level, at grade level, and above grade level. If possible, have nonfiction easy readers and wordless picture books. Encourage students to scan books that are beyond their current reading ability; this enables them to review the greatest number of topics before selecting one. You may be able to enlarge your classroom book selection through the school library or even the public library. Some public libraries will loan large quantities of materials to teachers for up to 30 days of classroom use.

Students may find research topics that interest them by referring to their own unanswered questions in their learning logs.

❖ Helping Students Establish Inquiry Questions

After students have identified an interesting topic, they need questions about it. Some may struggle to come up with questions. If this happens, prompt them with questions such as, "What would you like to know more about? What are some things that interest you? Do you collect anything? What are some questions you have about how things work?" Thought-provoking questions are the most suitable for inquiry, but students need adequate time to think of them. When they start their research they may not have enough background knowledge to pose any meaningful questions. Guide them by modeling questions you have about the subject.

Strategies: The Research Process

⊹ The Research Process

One way to introduce independent research in third grade is to allow the children to do research as partners, pairing a strong reader with a weaker one whenever possible. First, generate some topics as a whole class that the students might be interested in exploring. Then, ask for volunteers to commit to each topic (more than one set of partners can be assigned to the same topic). Now, ask each pair to come up with two queries they want to investigate. In this way, there will be topic differentiation in the pairs with the same topic.

Whether done as a whole group or independently, the research process follows these steps:

1. **Planning**—Establish deadlines for inquiry questions, information gathering, categorizing and classifying, first draft, second draft, final copy, and the final presentation/publication.

2. **Questioning**—Students determine the questions they want to investigate and then ask, "Where should I go or whom should I ask for information?"

3. **Gathering and recording information**—Don't encourage children to avoid works "beyond" their reading abilities. If the child is motivated, just looking at the pictures and decoding a few captions can teach him or her a lot. To allow your students the greatest access to materials, record nonfiction books on tape (or have older students do so). Encourage them to use videos and audio tapes or to engage in research with the assistance of parents or older siblings. Students should use secondary sources and, if possible, one primary source. Secondary sources include print, electronic or other media. Primary sources include personal letters, interviews, surveys, and field trips. Require that students use at least three different resources. They can record information in any way that appeals to them.

4. **Analyzing**—Students determine what information to include and the order of presentation.

5. **Putting it all together**—Students establish a format for their individual presentations (page of class book, written report, guided imagery, jackdaw, readers' theater, etc.). This step includes writing/creating, revising, critiquing, and editing to perfect the final product.

6. **Sharing findings with others**—Students publish or present their final products to classmates, another class, parents, administrator, or volunteer adults.

Strategies: Schedule; Conducting Research; Writing Process; Presentation

✛ Research Schedule

In-depth inquiry projects take your most precious resource: time. However, it is time well spent. Your class might complete only three inquiry projects during an academic year. Keep in mind that three well-done in-depth projects are more educationally beneficial for your students than six hastily done ones.

To help you and your students pace yourselves, set deadlines for:

- selection of a topic and inquiry questions
- end of research phase
- first draft
- second draft
- final draft
- presentation

For independent researchers: Create a contract that states the student's name, topic, two or three in-depth inquiry questions (they cannot have simple yes or no answers), and the five deadline dates. Send the contract home and ask both students and parents to sign and return it to you.

✛ Conducting Research

The class brainstorms a list of topics and votes to determine which one to pursue. As students begin their research, show them how to skim material before deciding to read something in depth. Demonstrate a variety of note-taking strategies. Let each student choose the method that seems to work best for him or her. Students search for information and take notes. They may generate additional questions and try to answer those as well. Meet with each student at least once during this time (choose those who appear to be struggling first) to evaluate if any interventions are necessary to promote success. Establish a presentation schedule and send out invitations. The students submit their first drafts.

For independent researchers: Post an example of proper citation form for bibliographic entries.

✛ Writing Process

During this time, students engage in peer editing and work at revising their projects (written reports, multimedia presentations, etc). A second draft is prepared. After last-minute polishing and revisions, the final project is due.

✛ Presentation

Each student is given an opportunity to present his or her final project or a portion of the class's presentation.

Doing Primary-Source Research

Before your students engage in primary research, explain that interviewers rarely ask questions that can be answered "yes" or "no." Instead, they ask questions that will draw an extended response. If possible, model an interview with another adult for your class. Demonstrate good interviewing techniques and questions by asking such questions as these:

1. How did you become an expert (or become interested) in your field?

2. What did you do in order to learn more about it?

3. Do you have any personal experiences or interesting stories you can share about your work?

4. Can you think of anyone else that I should talk to about this topic?

Follow up by having each student choose an area in which he or she has expertise (such as cartoons or skateboarding) and conduct mock interviews with students practicing interview questions and techniques on each other. Once your students know how to ask the right kinds of questions of experts, help them to find the experts by using the phone book:

- Discuss the purpose and organization of each part and where to look for information (the White Pages are used if you already know the name of someone).

- Show the students the alphabetizing and guide words used to organize information in the Yellow Pages.

- Help students to realize that the information is there—they just need to identify the correct label. They will need help thinking of multiple guide words for a category. For example, a third grade student was researching landfills. For his primary research, he wanted to talk with someone in a garbage collection company. After looking in the Yellow Pages under "trash" and "garbage" and finding nothing, he was stumped. His teacher suggested looking under "refuse." It wasn't there, but under refuse they found a notation to look under "rubbish collection."

Primary-Source Strategies: Surveys

❖ Surveys

Some students will conduct surveys for their primary source information. They should select an audience (their class, the entire fifth grade in your school, a neighborhood) and choose questions. To carry out this research, the students need to know how to record responses with tick marks, tabulate the responses, and then create graphs to show the results. They must include the conclusions drawn from the results in their final project.

Primary-Source Strategies: Surveys *(cont.)*

Be sure to provide examples and an explanation of when to use each type of graph:

Bar graphs and **pictographs** are useful for comparing items and are the two types of graphs that are the easiest for students to read and create.

Bar Graph

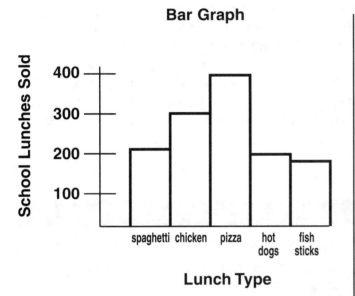

Conclusions: Pizza is the most popular lunch. Fish sticks are the least popular lunch.

Pictograph

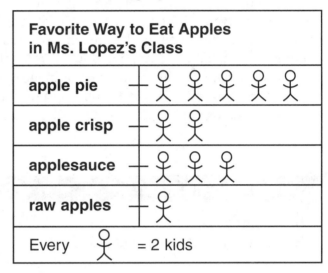

Conclusions: Each way was chosen by at least 2 people. Apple pie was the favorite and raw apples were the least favorite.

Line graphs show a trend or changes over time.

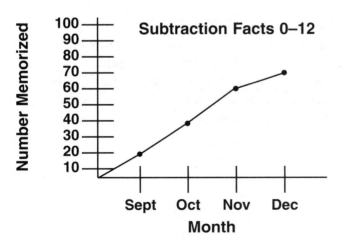

Conclusion: I am memorizing about 20 more subtraction facts each month!

Pie graphs show parts of a whole using percentages; they are usually too advanced for primary students to create.

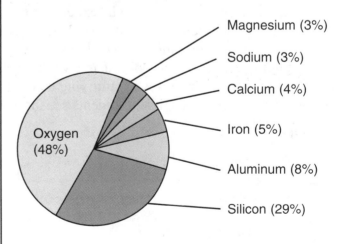

Major Elements in the Earth's Crust

Primary-Source Strategies: Community of Learners

✛ A Community of Learners

Inquiry thrives in a community of learners. Think of how often you've looked to others for recommendations on a good plumber, podiatrist, beautician, etc. Word of mouth is so powerful that businesses thrive or fail largely because of it. Plus, firsthand information is sometimes the most interesting. Capitalize on this by creating a bulletin board to enable students and adults to share their expertise. Locate the bulletin board in a central place to which both students and faculty have access. Each student can write his or her area of inquiry, name, teacher's name, and grade in one column. The second column provides space for others to respond with their names and how to contact them. The following is an example:

Can You Tell Me About...	Yes! Here's how to contact me:
orangutans Shauna Williams, Mr. Smith, gr. 3	Mrs. DeSalma Leave me a message in my mailbox in the main office.
steam engines Rja Adul, Ms. Sadowski, gr. 2	Mr. Morton, custodian Come see me. I'm in my office every day before school.
hang gliding Damon Walker, Mrs. Argast, gr. 1	Yvette Fernandez, Mr. Yunker's grade 6 Call me at 555–0987 after school.

You may be surprised at how much "expertise" exists within your school family. Someone's dad may work with the poisonous snakes at a local zoo. A fifth grader may have researched and prepared a presentation on hot air balloons. The librarian may be a Harley-Davidson motorcycle enthusiast. Send home a notice with a list of topics that haven't received any responses. In this way, you can involve parents and extended relatives by notifying them of a need for expertise they may possess. Not only is this good public relations, it lets students see those around them in a new light. Everyone is an expert at something.

Doing Secondary-Source Research

Teach your students that books with older copyright dates are not necessarily bad; however, new information found in the meantime may have rendered them obsolete. Historical events are usually described accurately even in an outdated publication, but this often isn't the case with science or technology. Also, make sure that your students realize that not everything is known or may ever be known about an ancient event or a person who lived long ago.

Secondary-Source Strategies: Library; Knowing Where to Find Answers

❖ Using the Library for Research

Before embarking on a research project, distribute grid paper and take the students to the school library. Have each student make a map of the library, indicating where these things are located:

- ◆ nonfiction books
- ◆ computers
- ◆ encyclopedias
- ◆ biographies

- ◆ CD-ROMs/videos
- ◆ magazines
- ◆ maps
- ◆ atlases

❖ Knowing Where to Find Answers

Students need to know where to search for answers to their questions. Gather together a collection of different styles of expository text. Look through them with your class. Ask students to identify the common elements in all nonfiction books. Then have students identify possible questions that they might ask about each book (does it have a glossary, index, table of contents, illustrations, etc.), its probability of answering a certain type of question, and where to look in the book for the answer to a question.

Students need to quickly analyze a source to determine its potential usefulness in answering research questions. To do so, students need a familiarity with where to look in a book for information (Bamford and Kristo, 2000). A simple exercise can present this information to them:

Directions: The left column lists different parts of reference books. The right column has things you may need to find out. Draw a line to match the part of the book where you would most likely find the information.

You want to know
1. in what year the book was published
2. whether George Eastman is mentioned in the book
3. the names of the chapters in the book
4. what the word "plateau" means

Book part
a. glossary
b. table of contents
c. copyright page
d. index

Answers: 1–c, 2–d, 3–b, 4–a

Secondary-Source Strategies: Computer; Organizing Materials; Recording Information

❖ Using a Computer for Research

Searching the Internet can consume too much time for too little benefit. Prevent this from happening by having students do Internet research only when:

- ✦ the information needs to be up-to-date (such as innovations in electric-hybrid cars)
- ✦ they cannot locate much information in other sources
- ✦ they need information from distant experts and can find a way to contact them via the Web
- ✦ the topic is too new to be in many print sources (such as recent discoveries of an anti-cancer agent discovered in an Amazon rain forest plant)

Show students how to limit a cybersearch. For example, entering "vaccine" as a topic may result in 235,489 hits; entering "smallpox vaccine" will result in fewer. They will need guidance in choosing alternative key words to use as search descriptors.

Post key rings with index cards attached at the computer. On each index card, write the topic, URL, and a brief description of a Web site that a student has found helpful. Continue to add new cards, maintaining alphabetical order based on topic. As these key ring collections grow over time, they can save your students a lot of time.

❖ Organizing Materials

Use individual mini baskets or cubbies for students to keep their research materials. Larger baskets are also ideal for text sets—nonfiction works about a particular topic written at a variety of reading levels (at, above, and below grade). If you purchase the small laundry-style baskets, be sure to get the 14 ¾"L x 10 ¼"W x 4 ⅓"H size, because many nonfiction books tend to be large.

❖ Recording Information

Research means taking notes. Demonstrate different ways to take notes and let each student choose his or her favorite method. In addition to the methods described in this section, students can use the Informal Notes Outline (page 152). To reduce the amount of writing necessary to record and share interesting discoveries, Blachowicz and Ogle (2001) recommend the use of the form on page 129:

Can you believe?

<u>The Northern Lights are caused by particles from the sun. It lights up the gases in our atmosphere. The gases glow different colors, like green, pink, and white.</u>

found by <u>Richard O. Gonzales</u> in <u>You Asked?</u>
      (child's name)   *(title)*

by <u>Katherine Farris</u>
    (author's name)

Lead a whole-group lesson to discuss and categorize these facts.

Secondary-Source Strategies: Recording Information *(cont.)*

Graphic Organizers

Can you believe?

_____

_____

found by _____ in _____
                   (your name)   *(title)*

by _____ .
              (author's name)

Can you believe?

_____

_____

found by _____ in _____
                    (your name)   *(title)*

by _____ .
              (author's name)

Can you believe?

_____

_____

found by _____ in _____
                    (your name)   *(title)*

by _____ .
               (author's name)

Secondary-Source Strategies: K-W-L Chart

❖ K-W-L Chart

A K-W-L chart (Ogle, 1986) offers an excellent format for research notes. Your students ask questions, come up with hypotheses (probable answers), and do research to determine if their theories are correct. With primary classes, do the K-W-L chart as a whole class. Create a large K-W-L chart on a board or butcher paper. Record student knowledge in the "I Know" column. Tape sentence strips with students' questions in the "I Wonder" column. At the end of the unit, peel off the questions and give one to each child in the class to answer. When he or she answers correctly, move the strip to the "I Learned" column.

For independent researchers: Distribute copies of page 131. Ask the students to write everything they already know about their topic in the "I Know" column. Then ask them to individually think of three research questions and write them in the "I Wonder" column. K-W-L charts enable you to maintain more control over the research process by reviewing the students' charts at these critical points:

- beginning (check the "I Know" column)

- after they've established the three queries (look at the "I Wonder" column)

- about midway through the time allotted for research (look at the "I Learned" column)

In the example below, the student is just starting her inquiry project. She has prepared a K-W-L chart about electricity by writing all that she knows about the subject in the "I Know" column. In the "I Wonder" column she has written four research questions followed by her theory in parentheses. She will fill in the "I Learned" column as she finds information.

I Know	I Wonder	I Learned
Electricity makes the lights and appliances work in my home.	What is an electrical circuit? (an outlet)	
Our house has circuit breakers.	What does a circuit breaker do? (keeps you from getting electrocuted)	
Lightning is a kind of electricity.	Can lightning be collected and used as electricity? (yes, in things like solar collectors)	
If you get electrocuted, you can die.	How can you get electrocuted? (by sticking something metal in an outlet)	

As you can see, this student has a lot of curiosity but not too much real knowledge about electricity. That's okay. She is motivated to find out more about a subject in which she is interested. Her questions will undoubtedly be answered through her research.

Strategies: K-W-L Chart *(cont.)*

Graphic Organizer

I Know	I Wonder	I Learned

Secondary-Source Strategies: Sum-It-Up Chart

⊹ Sum-It-Up Chart

A Sum-It-Up Chart (page 133) is a great way for students to record notes. Have students use a separate Sum-It-Up Chart for each reference work. Here is an example:

Look for	Answer	Source
who or what	Pilgrims	*2001 World Book Encyclopedia* on CD-ROM. Ivid Communications and IBM Corporation, 2001.
did what	had first Thanksgiving	
when	during fall 1621	
where	Plymouth, Massachusetts	
why	to thank God for their lives and crops in the new land	
how	had a really big meal	

Write a sentence or two that sums up the information in the chart:

The Pilgrims had the first Thanksgiving in Plymouth, Massachusetts, during the fall of 1621. They had a big meal in order to thank God for their lives and crops in the new land.

Secondary-Source Strategies: Sum-It-Up Chart *(cont.)*

Graphic Organizer

Look for	Answer	Source
who or what		
did what		
when		
where		
why		
how		

Write a sentence or two that sums up the information in the chart.

_____

_____

_____

_____

Secondary-Source Strategies: Query Chart

✥ Query Chart

Query charts (Hoffman, 1992) are an excellent way for students to find answers to questions, to learn that different authors highlight different material about a subject, and to discover that "facts" are sometimes disputed. In addition, by studying things from more than one perspective, students become accustomed to looking at events from more than one viewpoint.

Bring in a variety of books on a specific topic. Read the books aloud, directing students to listen for facts. Note these on a query chart on a large sheet of butcher paper. Discuss how you can determine definite facts (more written sources, college professors or community experts, etc.), but explain that there will be times when no one knows the answer for certain (and perhaps never will). For example, the exact date of Harriett Tubman's birth will never be known since no records were kept of slave births.

Initial query charts should be done on large sheets of construction paper to allow space for children's handwriting. Independent researchers can fill out the query chart on page 135.

Topic: The Loch Ness monster	Query: What does it look like?	Query: What is it?
Resource 1: *2001 World Book Encyclopedia* on CD-ROM	• 20 to 30 feet long • four flippers • tiny head • long, thin neck • one, two, or three humps on back	• a modern kind of plesiosaur (a swimming dinosaur) • an unknown kind of huge water snake
Resource 2: *The Loch Ness Monster* by Ellen Rabinowich	• long neck • little head • two small horns • over 40 feet long • one or two humps on its back	• a huge sea cow (manatee) • an unknown type of sea serpent • a giant eel • a plesiosaur
Resource 3: *Monster Mysteries* by Rupert Matthews	• 1975 underwater photo shows outline of a big animals with flippers	• an unknown kind of water worm • a descendant of a plesiosaur
Sum-up	It seems to have a long neck, small head, flippers, and a hump.	Many people think it is a plesiosaur (swimming dinosaur).
New Queries	Who has seen the monster?	Are there any more recent discoveries or proof?

Secondary-Source Strategies: Query Chart *(cont.)*

Graphic Organizer

Topic:	Query:	Query:
Resource 1:		
Resource 2:		
Resource 3:		
Sum-up		
New Queries		

Secondary-Source Strategies: Web Notes

✥ Web Notes

The youngest students may find it easiest to record notes in a semantic web. This lets them use drawings to help them process the material. Note how the web the child drew for this information incorporates the details with both physical placement and pictures.

> North, south, east, and west are directions. North is the opposite of south. East is the opposite of west. You can tell directions based on the sun. The sun rises in the east. If the rising sun is on your right, you are facing north. The sun sets in the west. If the setting sun is on your right, you are facing south.

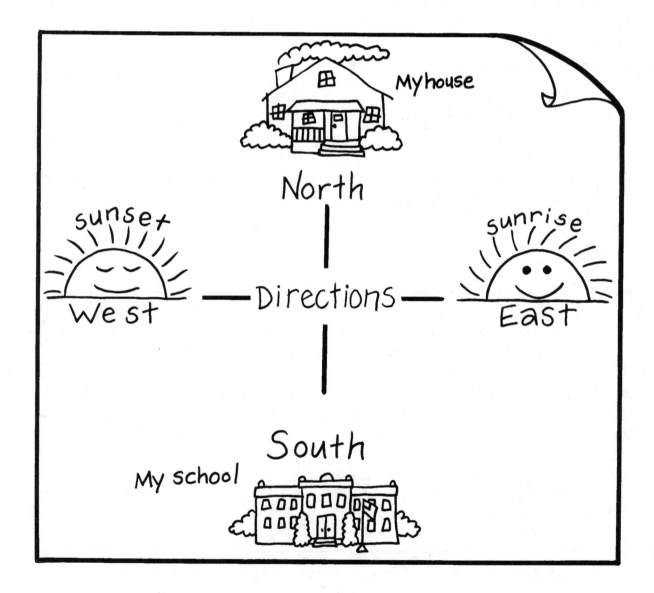

Research-Project Strategies: Pattern Report; Written Reports; Guided Imagery

✛ Pattern Report

Students can share their nonfiction knowledge by following a comfortable, familiar pattern from a storybook. Read aloud Bill Martin's *Brown Bear, Brown Bear, What Do You See?* (Henry Holt and Company, 1996) or *Polar Bear, Polar Bear, What Do You Hear?* (Henry Holt and Company, 1997). Then have the children follow his format to dictate or write their own reports. Here's the portion in a report on pioneers about the sounds of the prairie:

> Pioneer, pioneer, what do you hear? I hear wagon wheels squeaking. That's what I hear. Wagon wheels, wagon wheels, what do you hear? I hear the wind blowing through the tall grass. That's what I hear. Tall grass, tall grass, what do you hear? I hear a wolf howling in the distance. That's what I hear. . . .

✛ Other Written Reports

For information on teaching beginning writers how to write nonfiction, refer to the Emerging Reading and Writing Skills section (pages 57–62) and the Writing Nonfiction section (pages 90–119).

Require at least one visual in any written report. For example, a student can draw to scale (by hand or computer) the relationship of the size of the classroom compared to the length of an Australian alligator; make a collage of pictures cut from magazines; create a drawing of a killer whale in its ocean habitat; make a time line of the development of the computer; or include photographs of recyclable items.

✛ Guided Imagery

Students can develop guided imagery exercises (Gambrell, et al., 1987) about their topics. Your students will learn a great deal both from preparing their own guided-imagery exercises and experiencing each other's. As the student guides the rest of the class through his or her guided-imagery exercise, you will be pleased by the classmates' rapt attention. Ideas are only as limited as your students' imaginations. Provide a list of ideas to the students, but also let them develop their own ideas. Students could do one of the following:

- ✦ Have the class wear blindfolds while a student talks them through a visualization of the topic (such as a day in the life of a polar bear).

- ✦ Tell a story (without pictures) that includes important facts about the topic. Students may use cue cards but cannot read aloud.

- ✦ Provide tactile props to help explain characteristics. A student reporting about eggs may have each person in the class stick his or her hand through the lid of four different shoe boxes. Inside each will be an example of a type of egg: one box will contain a hard-boiled chicken egg; another a jar of jelly (for fish, toad, and frog eggs); another, shampoo (for certain types of insect eggs); and the final box could have a leaf with insect eggs actually implanted in it.

- ✦ Write a poem or song that includes all the pertinent information and perform it for the class.

Research-Project Strategies: Jackdaws

⁜ Jackdaws

A jackdaw is a bird that hoards things in its nest. A jackdaw project is a collection of things related to a specific topic. These projects promote higher-level thinking skills in an enjoyable way. Students prepare a card for each item in the box, explaining its significance. Here is a student's jackdaw about the state of Arizona:

✧ cup of sand (desert)

✧ quartz (Petrified Forest)

✧ telescope (Lowell Observatory)

✧ pine twigs (Ponderosa pines)

✧ clay with crater (Barrington Crater)

Citing Resources

Third graders can be expected to cite their sources in this manner:

✧ **Book**
Author's first name and last name. <u>Title of work</u>. Year.
Example: Debra Housel. <u>Developing Listening Skills</u>. 2001.

✧ **CD-ROM**
<u>Title of CD-ROM</u>. CD-ROM, year.
Example: <u>2001 World Book Encyclopedia</u>. CD-ROM, 2001.

✧ **Magazine or newspaper article**
Author's name. "Title of article." <u>Title of magazine</u>. Date.
Example: Brenda Power. "Talk in the Classroom." <u>Scholastic Instructor</u>. September 2001.

✧ **Video/film**
<u>Title of film</u>. Type of film. Publisher, year.
Example: <u>The Grizzlies</u>. Videotape. National Geographic Video, 1987.

✧ **Web site**
Name of Web site. URL.
Example: Teacher Created Materials. www.teachercreated.com

(**Note:** If students are using a computer, all the underlined items should be italicized instead.)

Introduction to Section 8: Remembering Nonfiction

Much of education relies upon memory. In today's educational environment, once a standard or benchmark is met at one level, the students are expected to build upon that knowledge. This means that they need to remember it.

What works to trigger one person's memory will not necessarily help another. This section details many ways that you can improve your students' ability to recall expository information. All of them have research-based proof that they increase memory. Try as many of them as you possibly can.

Strategies: Songs and Rhymes; Acronyms; Five Fingers

❖ Songs and Rhymes

Singing information helps commit it to permanent memory. One example of the power of song came from an informal study of college students who had memorized the 50 states and their capitals. After five years, the only students who had retained all of the information were those who had been taught to sing the states and their capitals.

Rhymes are powerful memory boosters, too. Many of us rely on the ancient rhyme, "Thirty Days Hath September" to determine how many days are in a particular month.

❖ Acronyms

Acronyms aid memorization. You may recognize "Roy G. Biv" as a common acronym for remembering the colors of the rainbow in order (red, orange, yellow, green, blue, indigo, and violet). Researchers have found individually created acronyms the most effective. The mental stimulation needed to think of an acronym helps put the information into long-term memory.

❖ Five Fingers

When students need to remember data sets with five elements, they can use their fingers to remember the information. Have students assign a piece of data to each finger on one hand. Since the student needs to know that there is one piece of data for each finger, this works only when you have data set of five. See the example provided to the right:

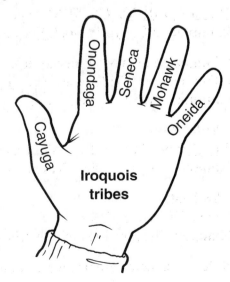

Iroquois tribes

Strategies: Text Response Centers

✣ Text Response Centers

Rotate your students through text response centers (Keene and Zimmerman, 1997) to create lasting impressions and encourage your students to use their multiple intelligences.

Drama—Students act out the events they have read about. They can write a script, assign and memorize parts, create puppets, and perform a puppet show for the class. They can also develop a readers' theater script or do pantomime. Provide the students with crayons, markers, yarn, fabric scraps, sequins, buttons, staples and stapler, glue, scissors, empty, paper-towel tubes (cut in half) or toilet paper tubes, and lots of photocopies of the puppet patterns on page 141. One child can manage two puppets (one on each index finger). Construct a stage from a large, empty cardboard box (appliance boxes work really well). Cut away the sides of the box until just three attached sides remain. Using the existing folds of the box, bend the sides so that they flare out. This will provide the puppeteers with elbow room. Cut out a window in the front of the box in one of two ways: leaving the "shutters" on so you can "close the curtain" by shutting them or cutting out a large window area and draping a cloth behind it, which the children move aside when performing. If you leave the shutters on, you will need to use Velcro™ on the back of the shutters and the front of the theater to hold the shutters wide open during performances.

Models—Students create models of their favorite image from information they heard or read. Provide chenille sticks (pipe cleaners); plenty of tagboard, oaktag, or sturdy cardboard; modeling clay in many colors; tape; glue stick; scissors; cotton balls; and craft sticks.

Writer's Nook—The students describe a strong or favorite image created by information. Provide lined paper, stapler and staples, pencils or pens of different colors, construction paper, glue, and scissors. Students can make a construction paper or oaktag frame for their written work and display it for others to read. They can also tape a lined sheet of paper to the bottom of the frame to give readers an opportunity to react to what the writer said.

Studio—Each student creates an artistic response to expository information. Supplies needed include different sizes of unlined paper, crayons, colored pencils, markers, glue stick, fabric scraps, string, scissors, watercolor paints, and brushes. The students can exhibit their artwork in the room or hall. They may tape a lined sheet of paper to the bottom of the frame to let viewers write their reactions to the artist's creation. Occasionally ask students to explain their work to the class, telling why they selected the media and colors they used to express their ideas.

Text Club—The purpose of the text club is to discuss what's been learned. To create a relaxed atmosphere conducive to conversation, have comfortable chairs or carpet squares, pretzels or saltines, and cups of water. Since nothing tangible gets produced at this center, tape record the discussions to keep the students on track. At a convenient time, you can listen to the tape to ensure the children are staying focused.

To let the students know that you value their creations and to show the rest of the class the type of things you want produced, randomly highlight student work from each center. For example, read aloud a Writer's Nook response and say, "I liked how John used red ink to write his response to the Native American treaties being repeatedly broken. It helps to show me that he understands the tribes' anger at not being able to rely on the government's promises."

Strategies: Text Response Centers *(cont.)*

Puppet Patterns

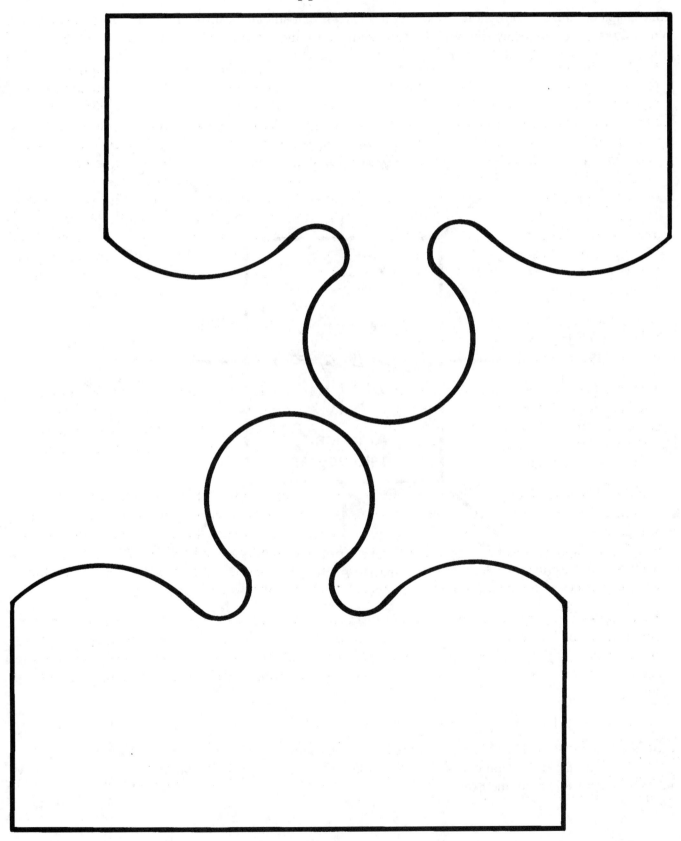

Strategies: Mind Maps

❖ Mind Maps

Mind maps organize information. Research has shown that students can often recall information stored in a mind map because they can readily visualize it. Introduce this technique using the graphic organizer on page 143 and the example below:

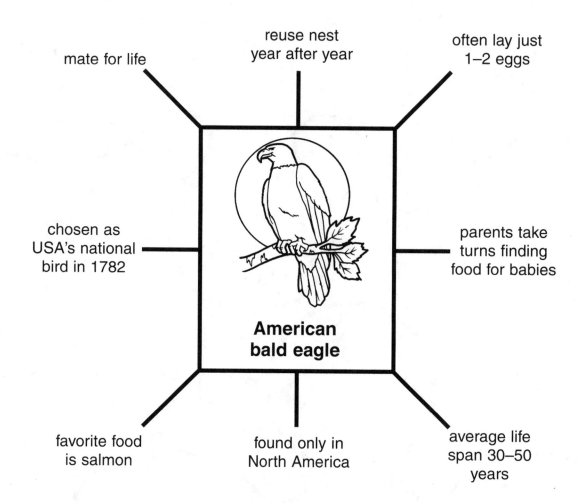

Show students how to create their own individual mind maps by demonstrating your thinking and the resulting mind map on several occasions. As students become more comfortable with mind maps, they may spontaneously create their own.

Strategies: Mind Map *(cont.)*

Graphic Organizer

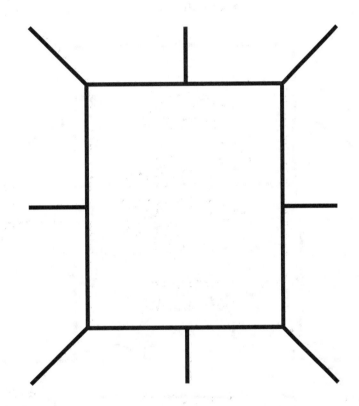

Strategies: Cycle Organizer

✛ Cycle Organizer

Students can remember a process using the cycle graphic organizer on page 145. This is particularly effective for the water cycle, rock cycle, or seasonal cycle. It's also good for the life cycles of plants, animals, or habitats (such as a forest). Here's an example:

Life Cycle of a Butterfly

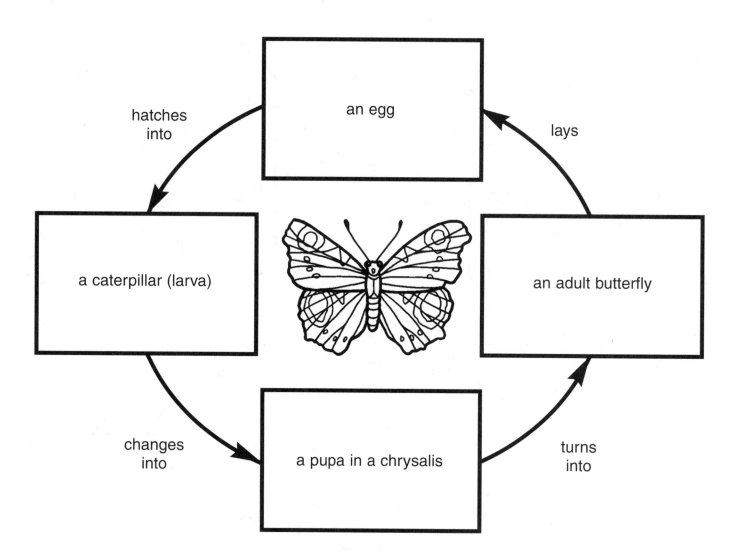

Strategies: Cycle Organizer (cont.)

Graphic Organizer

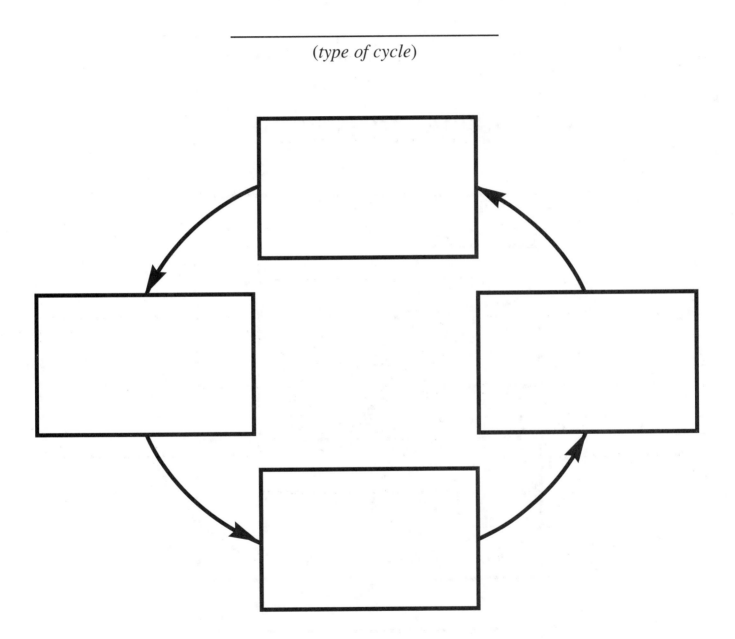

_____

(type of cycle)

Strategies: Step-by-Step Organizer

❖ Step-by-Step Organizer

Students can remember the steps in a process or event by using the step-by-step graphic organizer on page 147. This is particularly effective for things that must occur in a specific order but do not cycle. Here is an example:

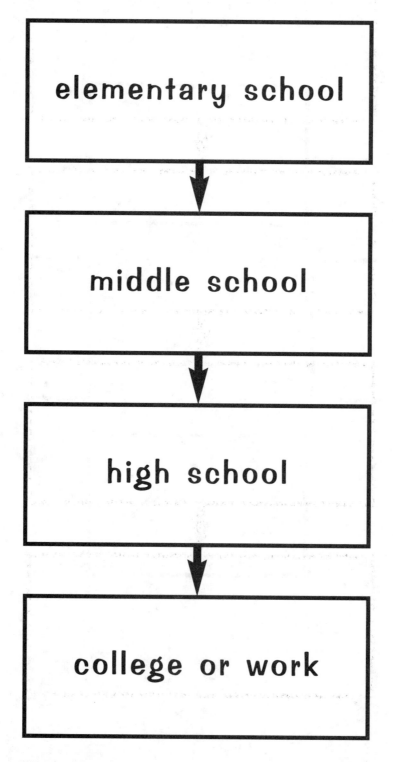

Strategies: Step-by-Step Organizer *(cont.)*

Graphic Organizer

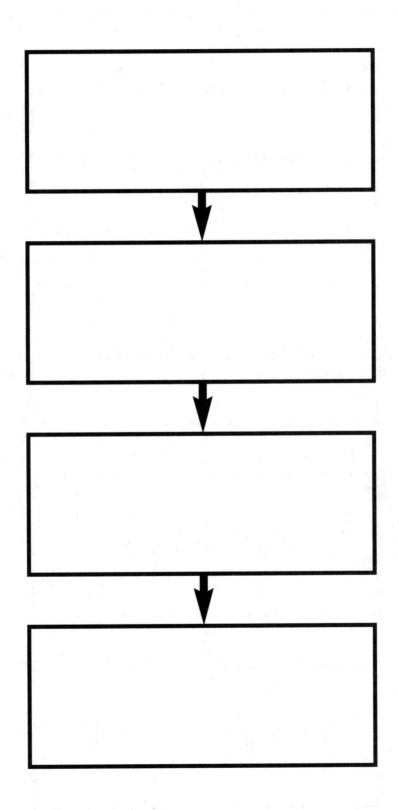

Strategies: Home-School Folder

❖ Home-School Folder

Create a home-school folder for each student. Send them home each week on Friday and ask parents to sign them and return them on Monday. On Friday, the students complete the form on page 149, adding it to the folder filled with that week's finished work. This gives them an opportunity to review and synthesize what's been learned that week as well as provide an opening for discussion with parents about school. When the forms are returned, keep them in each student's folder or portfolio as a record of learning throughout the year.

Dear Parent,

This is what happened this week. Please read it and sign it. I must return it on Monday.

In **math**, I learned about place value for big numbers using cube sticks.	In **science**, I learned how different animals have babies.
In **social studies**, we talked about how communities around the world (neighborhoods and towns) are similar.	In **language arts**, we read *Freckle Juice* and learned some common word endings. I also did research for my inquiry project on dolphins.
This is how I did: ___G___ Following directions ___I___ Listening ___I___ Keeping my stuff neat ___V___ Participating in class **V = Very good** **G = Good** **I = I need to improve**	**Parent signature and comments:** You really covered a lot in just one week. I'm proud of you! *Edelia J. Lopez*

Strategies: Home-School Folder *(cont.)*

Graphic Organizer

Dear Parent,   Week of _____

This is a summary of my week. Please read it, write a comment, and sign it. I must return it on Monday.

In **math**,	In **science**,

In **social studies**,	In **language arts**,

This is how I did:

_____ Following directions
_____ Listening
_____ Keeping my stuff neat
_____ Turning in work on time
_____ Participating in class

V = Very good
G = Good
I = I need to improve

Parent comments:

Strategies: Bare Bones

✣ Bare Bones Summary

A bare bones summary works best when used with a short expository passage. (If you use it with a longer passage, be sure to provide students with additional copies of the graphic organizer on page 151.) Have students read a passage and then identify the minimum number of words that will carry the message. They record the words or phrases in order, resulting in the "bare bones" of information. When studying the graphic organizer, the students exercise their memories by having to "flesh out" the details. For example, the students read this passage and create this bare bones summary:

People have hurt the Amazon rain forest. They have taken away dirt to look for gold. Millions of trees are cut down for furniture. Many more plants and animals become extinct every day.

People Hurt the Amazon Rain Forest

take away soil

cut down trees

plants and animals become extinct

Strategies: **Bare Bones** *(cont.)*

Graphic Organizer

Strategies: Informal Notes

✤ Informal Notes Outline

Outlines contain the main ideas and important details from a text. Working as a whole class, primary students can fill in the informal outline on page 153. The following is an example:

Stars are not all the same size. Some are big. Some are small. Some give more light than others do. The sun is a star. It isn't the biggest one. It just looks like the biggest because it is closer to Earth than the other stars.

Here's how the outline would look for this paragraph for each of the different grades:

Grade 1: You provide all of the details; students must identify the main idea.

Main Idea: _____

D1: _____Some stars are big._____

D2: _____Some stars are small._____

D3: _____Our sun is a star._____

D4: _____The sun looks so big because it's close to Earth._____

Grade 2: You give the main idea and two details; the students must provide the other details.

Main Idea: __Stars are not all the same size._____

D1: __Some stars are big._____

D2: _____

D3: __Our sun is a star._____

D4: _____

Grade 3: You provide one detail; students must supply the main idea and all other details.

Main Idea: _____

D1: _____

D2: _____

D3: _____

D4: __The sun looks so big because it's close to Earth._____

Giving primary students practice with this strategy provides a solid foundation for the upper grades, when they will be expected to prepare informal outlines as they read nonfiction passages.

Strategies: Informal Notes (cont.)

Graphic Organizer

Main Idea: _____

    D1: _____

    D2: _____

    D3: _____

    D4: _____

Main Idea: _____

    D1: _____

    D2: _____

    D3: _____

    D4: _____

Main Idea: _____

    D1: _____

    D2: _____

    D3: _____

    D4: _____

Main Idea: _____

    D1: _____

    D2: _____

    D3: _____

    D4: _____

Strategies: Alphabet Book

⁛ Class Alphabet Book

A class alphabet book compiles terms, facts, or events related to a topic. Make an overhead transparency of page 155. As a class, brainstorm words or phrases for each letter related to a specific topic. Record the information. Then photocopy the completed graphic organizer and distribute it to the students.

Directions: Write a word or a phrase that relates to the topic and begins with each letter.

Topic: Math Words	A addition adding answer	B bigger bar graph	C count cubes cents calculator	D dime divide decimal dollar	E equal to eight	F four five fraction
G graph greater than	H how many hundred half	I inches	J joining sets	K keep in order	L less than line graph	M minus sign many more than measure
N numbers nickel	O odd numbers one	P plus sign pie graph pictograph penny	Q question quarter	R right answer	S subtract square sets six seven	T triangle two three then thousand
U up under	V volume	W word problem wrong answer	X explain	Y yardstick	Z zero	

Pair the students and have them prepare four pages, including explanations and illustrations. Assign each pair one easy and one harder letter (such as C and I). Allows words that begin with the letters "ex" for X. Have students sketch rough drafts and verify their information with you before preparing the final copies of their pages. Post an example of how each page should look:

A is for "Add." We add two numbers and get a bigger number. $6 + 4 = 10$ 10 is bigger than 6. 10 is bigger than 4.	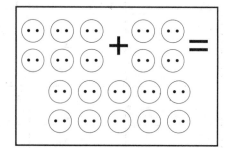

Combine the pages into a published class book. Find a way for other students to access the book upon its completion, perhaps by placing it in the school library's circulating collection.

Strategies: Alphabet Book *(cont.)*

Graphic Organizer

Directions: Write a word or a phrase that relates to the topic and begins with each letter.

Topic:	A	B	C	D	E	F
G	H	I	J	K	L	M
N	O	P	Q	R	S	T
U	V	W	X	Y	Z	

Introduction to Section 9: Assessing Nonfiction Comprehension

Although every instructional activity can be used for assessment, this section provides you with additional ways to determine your students' educational progress.

The purpose of assessment is to let you know the specific instruction your students need. Knowing this increases your instructional time because you don't spend time going over what your students already know. Authentic assessment lets you pinpoint each student's specific strengths, weaknesses, and misconceptions. This type of evaluation tells you, the student, and the parents more useful information than a "C+" or a "76." Effective authentic assessment tools include:

- portfolios
- performances
- scoring guides

- educator observation and checklists
- student self-assessment

Strategies: Portfolios; Performances

✛ Portfolios

A portfolio is a collection of each student's work and academic development over time. Each student's portfolio showcases his or her best pieces of work throughout the school year. Make portfolios a collaborative effort between you and each student; decide together what things to include. To reduce the bulk of a single portfolio, you may want to keep separate portfolios for each student in each content area.

Portfolio pieces are limited only by space and imagination. They can include a graph of student progress (such as fluency in terms of words read per minute), journals, word problems, samples of a student's written work, videotapes, his or her portion of group projects, and computer-generated assignments (such as a KidPix™ presentation on a CD).

✛ Performances

Performances are tangible products: tests, reports, projects, presentations, or oral recitations. A good performance assessment is to have each student individually read an unfamiliar nonfiction piece aloud at four points throughout the school year (such as the end of each quarter). At the same time have them do a writing sample. Store these performances in chronological order on a disk as a record of growth and learning to share with students, parents, and administrators.

For a more in-depth assessment, tape record a more extensive student performance. Have the student preview an unfamiliar text, then make a prediction and mention something he or she already knows about the topic. Have the student read the passage aloud and then orally summarize the passage after reading.

Strategies: Scoring Guides; Checklists; Self-Assessment

⁜ Scoring Guides

Scoring guides are a set of standards for measuring student skills. Scoring guides provide an accurate measure of student performance by having you assess each part of a student's work to determine an overall grade. Before beginning a task, go over the scoring guide with the class so that they know what's expected of them. The following scoring guides are provided:

- ✦ **Oral Retelling** (page 167)—Model for the students how to give an oral summary. Establish a system for randomly drawing students' names, such as craft sticks kept in a mug or names on slips of paper in a shoebox. After an expository reading, pick a student name and ask him or her to summarize or retell.

- ✦ **Written Retelling** (page 168)—Allow two readings of the material, but no access to the text while the student is composing the retelling. Emphasize that ideas count more than spelling or mechanics.

- ✦ **Discussion** (page 169)—Fill out this assessment for each student at least three times a year.

- ✦ **Research and Written Report** (page 170)

- ✦ **Research and Presentation** (page 171)

⁜ Educator Observation Checklists

Educator observation checklists help you to notice and record student behaviors that indicate competence or difficulty. A checklist gives you quick, efficient documentation of the specific skills a student has mastered. The conclusions drawn from such checklists are consistent and reliable if you use many observations over a period of time. Checklists are a good way for you to show students the areas on which they still need to work as well as those in which they excel. They also offer a meaningful way to discuss with parents the standards and benchmarks as they relate to their child's abilities. A comprehensive checklist of receptive skills (reading and listening) is provided on page 172, and a checklist of expressive skills (writing, speaking, and research) is given on page 173.

⁜ Student Self-Assessment

Students need to take an active role in their own assessment. Asking students to evaluate their own performances helps them to identify what they've done well and what they could improve. Page 174 has two student self-assessment tools. Students complete the top self-evaluation form after a unit of nonfiction study. Students fill out the bottom self-evaluation form after completing a major project or report. You may want to send these self-evaluation forms home for a parent to sign before storing them in the students' portfolios.

Strategies: Retellings; Alleviating Anxiety; Assessing Instruction

✢ Oral and Written Retellings

Provide a tape recorder. Have the students state their names and then retell all that they can recall about a nonfiction passage that they have chorally read or heard twice. They cannot refer to the passage during the retelling. Review the tape at a convenient time and use the oral retellings scoring guide on page 167 to evaluate it.

To ease the burden of oral retelling assessment with young children, have the children listen to or read a passage at the end of the day. When they go home, ask them to orally summarize the information for a parent, who records the summary verbatim and returns it to school. Since the parents never see the passage, you will get only information from the student.

If your students are capable of a written retelling, use the scoring guide on page 168. Allow the student at least two readings of the material but no access to the text while composing the retelling. Emphasize that only ideas count and that no points will be deducted for misspellings, grammar, and mechanics.

✢ Alleviating Test Anxiety

Many students feel anxious when told in advance that "this is a test" or "this is for a grade"—yet you cannot hide from students when and how they will be evaluated. One easy way to alleviate test anxiety is to always call tests "opportunities." Explain to the students that a test is merely an opportunity for them to show you what they know and for you to find out what you still need to teach. This simple explanation and renaming often goes a long way toward reducing your students' test anxiety.

✢ Assessing Your Instruction

Looking at the results of your students' opportunities is one way to assess your instruction. You can also evaluate the strategies that you use by keeping field notes. Field notes include three parts:

✦ a description of how you implemented the strategy

✦ how the students responded to the strategy

✦ why and how you modified the strategy (if you did so)

Strategies: Elements of a Set; Maze

❖ Identifying the Elements of a Set

Select the concepts to assess and create activities like these:

Circle the word in each group that contains the others:

Set 1	**Set 2**	**Set 3**
March	today	weekday
April	yesterday	Monday
month	tomorrow	Friday
June	day	Thursday

Color the box with the word that doesn't belong:

August	December
February	Wednesday

Extend this activity by asking students to write a brief explanation why the item doesn't belong.

❖ Maze

Maze practice, a variation on the cloze technique, offers an effective assessment of students' ability to rely on context when reading expository material. Select a passage from an expository text the students have not read but that is about the topic you have been studying. Re-type the passage to look like this example, omitting three to five words. For each omission, give three choices for the correct answer. Make certain that you leave blanks that are all the same size. For example:

Wolves live in groups. They "talk" to each other. They do this by _____.
(speaking, howling, whistling)

Often more than one wolf howls at a time. Each group has its own area of land. They

want other wolves to stay off their _____. So they howl to tell other wolves
(land, tails, food)

to stay away.

Wolves use other howls to say _____ things. They can howl to call
(angry, scary, different)

to stray group members together to go _____. Their howls may tell of
(swimming, hunting, sleeping)

danger. Sometimes, wolves even howl just because they are happy!

Strategies: Equation

⁜ Main Idea and Supporting Details: Equation

Students may find it helpful if you post this mathematical formula and example:

Detail 1 + Detail 2 + Detail 3 = Main Idea

Evaluate your students' ability to identify the main idea and find supporting details with the assessment tool on page 161. Provide the students with an unfamiliar nonfiction passage written at their independent reading level. Here's an example:

Read. Write a detail in each of the three small boxes. The details add up to the main idea. Write the main idea in the biggest box.

| The queen bee lays all of the eggs. | + | Worker bees collect honey, build the hive, and take care of the queen. | + | The drone bees fertilize the queen's eggs. | = |

In a hive, the three kinds of bees do different jobs.

Strategies: Equation (cont.)

Graphic Organizer

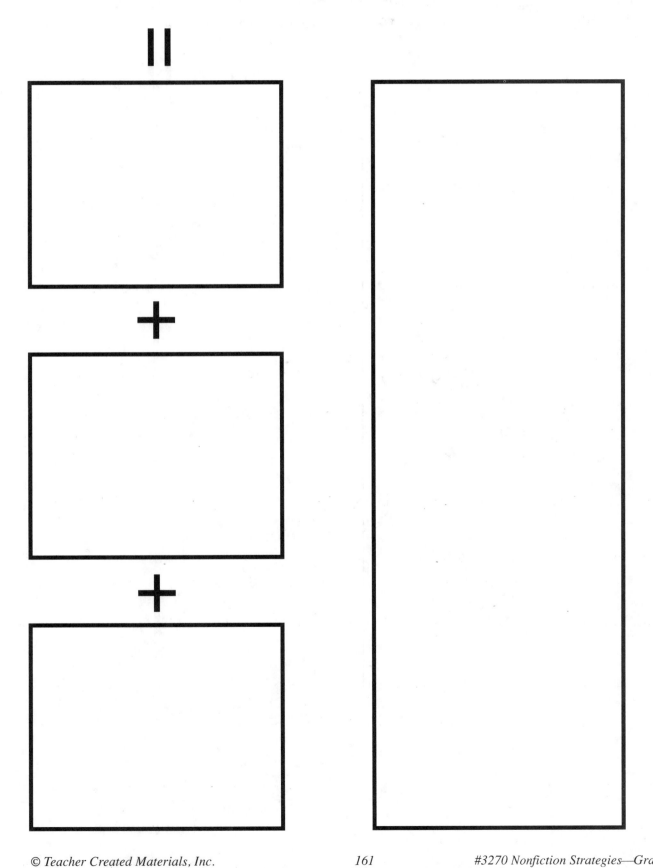

Strategies: Herringbone

A graphic organizer that allows students to quickly display their knowledge of who, what, when, where, why, and how is the herringbone (Tierney, Readence, and Dishner, 1990), named for a fish skeleton. Blank copies of the herringbone graphic organizer are provided on page 163. This is an example of a herringbone:

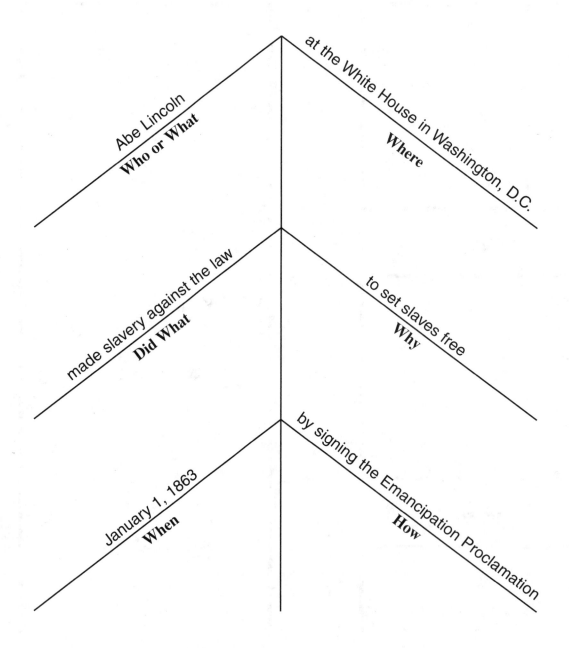

Strategies: Herringbone (cont.)

Graphic Organizer

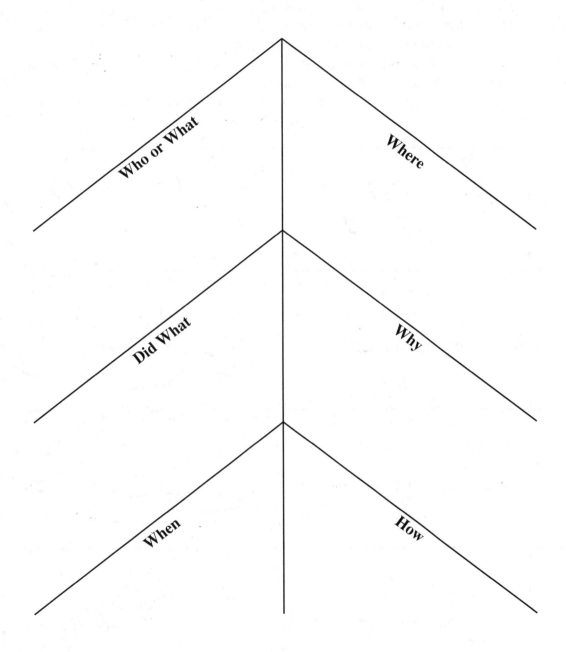

Strategies: Acrostic Grid

✥ Acrostic Grid

Copy the acrostic grid on page 165. Write the topic down the edge. Have students fill in the spaces with a word or phrase that starts with that letter and fits the category. Allow "ex" words for the letter X. Because primary students can often think of a word or phrase that begins with a letter but can not spell it, have them support their responses by drawing pictures in the box to depict what their words mean. When you first introduce this activity, do the acrostic grid as a whole class, then move to completing it in pairs. Eventually some children may be able to do this independently. Here's an example:

W	wet	
A	air holds water in clouds	
T	turns into ice or snow	
E	evaporates into the air	
R	rain brings water down to the ground	

Strategies: Acrostic Grid *(cont.)*

Graphic Organizer

Directions: In each space put a word or a phrase that begins with the letter and relates to the topic. You can draw pictures to show what you mean.

Strategies: Before-and-After Drawings

❖ Before-and-After Drawings

Give students large, unlined pieces of white drawing paper and have them draw what they know about a subject before studying it. For example, if you are going to read about our solar system, ask the students to draw what they think our solar systems looks like.

Pre-reading Drawing:

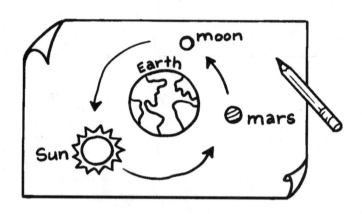

Post-reading Drawing:

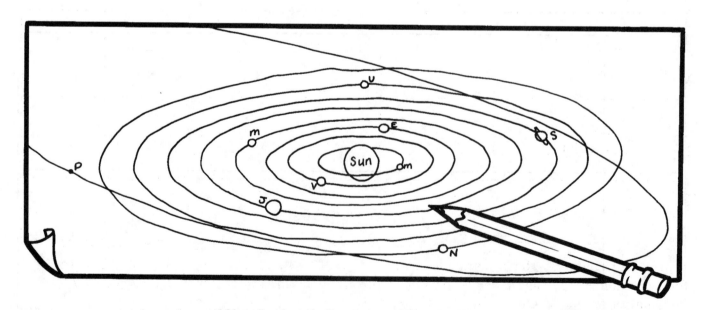

You can see that this student revised his or her mental image to include the correct number of planets and have them rotate around the sun.

Oral Retelling Scoring Guide

Behavior	Definitely (3 pt)	Usually (2 pt)	Sometimes (1 pt)	Not Yet (0 pt)	Points
States the main idea					
Includes all of the important information					
Omits irrelevant information					
Groups related ideas together					
Recalls facts accurately					
Tells events in sequence					
Speaks clearly and audibly					
				Total	

Scoring Instructions: Record 3 points for each "Definitely," 2 points for each "Usually," 1 point for each "Sometimes," and 0 points for each "Not Yet." Total the points column and divide by 7 (the number of areas evaluated) to receive an overall assessment score.

Overall Assessment Score: _____

Written Retelling Scoring Guide

Behavior	Definitely (3 pt)	Usually (2 pt)	Sometimes (1 pt)	Not Yet (0 pt)	Points
States the main idea					
Includes all of the important information					
Omits irrelevant information					
Groups related ideas together					
Recalls facts accurately					
Tells events in sequence					
Uses spelling and mechanics appropriate for the child's developmental level					
				Total	

Scoring Instructions: Record 3 points for each "Definitely," 2 points for each "Usually," 1 point for each "Sometimes," and 0 points for each "Not Yet." Total the points column and divide by 7 (the number of areas evaluated) to receive an overall assessment score.

Overall Assessment Score: _____

Discussion Scoring Guide

Behavior	Definitely (3 pt)	Usually (2 pt)	Sometimes (1 pt)	Not Yet (0 pt)	Points
States own ideas					
Listens to what others say					
Adds to what others have said					
Speaks clearly and audibly					
Sticks to the topic					
Takes turns speaking					
				Total	

Scoring Instructions: Record 3 points for each "Definitely," 2 points for each "Usually," 1 point for each "Sometimes," and 0 points for each "Not Yet." Total the points column and divide by 6 (the number of areas evaluated) to receive an overall assessment score.

Overall Assessment Score: _____

Research and Written Report
Scoring Guide

Behavior	Definitely (3 pt)	Usually (2 pt)	Sometimes (1 pt)	Not Yet (0 pt)	Points
Poses research questions					
Uses several appropriate resources					
Includes only important and relevant information					
Presents information in an organized, logical sequence					
Uses spelling and mechanics appropriate for the child's developmental level					
Includes a relevant visual					
Follows the proper format for a bibliography					
				Total	

Scoring Instructions: Record 3 points for each "Definitely," 2 points for each "Usually," 1 point for each "Sometimes," and 0 points for each "Not Yet." Total the points column and divide by 7 (the number of areas evaluated) to receive an overall assessment score.

Overall Assessment Score: _____

Research and Presentation Scoring Guide

Behavior	Definitely (3 pt)	Usually (2 pt)	Sometimes (1 pt)	Not Yet (0 pt)	Points
Poses research questions					
Uses several appropriate resources					
Includes only important, relevant facts					
Presents information in an organized, logical sequence					
Speaks clearly and audibly					
Includes a relevant visual					
Answers audience questions					
Follows the proper format for a bibliography					
				Total	

Scoring Instructions: Record 3 points for each "Definitely," 2 points for each "Usually," 1 point for each "Sometimes," and 0 points for each "Not Yet." Total the points column and divide by 8 (the number of areas evaluated) to receive an overall assessment score.

Overall Assessment Score: _____

Nonfiction Receptive Skills Checklist

Name: _____   Date: _____

A = almost always   **S = sometimes**   **N = not yet**

Receptive Skills (Reading and Listening)	Rating
Reads grade-level nonfiction text independently.	
Previews texts to set a purpose for reading.	
Relates prior knowledge and experiences to understand and respond to new information.	
Makes, confirms, and revises predictions throughout the reading process.	
Monitors own comprehension while reading.	
Uses different strategies to tackle unknown words or difficult concepts.	
Creates mental images from pictures and print.	
Identifies the main idea and supporting details of expository text.	
Locates requested information in a passage.	
Recalls facts from what's been read.	
Understands simple maps, tables, and graphs included in passage.	
Uses picture clues to make inferences and draw conclusions.	
Shows critical and reflective thinking about the messages in text.	
Asks questions before, during, and after reading.	
Actively listens to nonfiction text.	
Visualizes while listening.	
Identifies facts in oral presentations.	
Listens to classmates during a discussion.	
Listens in order to understand a speaker's topic.	

Nonfiction Expressive Skills Checklist

Name: _____   Date: _____

A = almost always   **S = sometimes**   **N = not yet**

Expressive Skills (Speaking and Writing)	Rating
Makes contributions in class and group discussions.	
Asks questions of teacher and others.	
Responds to questions and comments.	
Conveys a clear main point when speaking to others.	
Stays on topic being discussed.	
Plays a variety of roles in small group discussions.	
Takes turns speaking in a discussion.	
Adds to what others say during a discussion.	
Retells sequential events in the correct order.	
Compares and contrasts information.	
Forms ideas, opinions, and personal responses to texts.	
Summarizes information effectively.	
Writes information in a logical order.	
Utilizes information-organizing strategies.	
Dictates or composes a simple research paper or presentation.	
Organizes ideas for oral presentations.	
Makes presentations in front of the class.	
Research Skills	**Rating**
Identifies topics to investigate.	
Establishes questions to be answered by research.	
Explores unfamiliar resources.	
Gather information about a topic using a variety of materials.	
Uses the parts of the book and text structure to find information.	
Uses graphic organizers to record information.	
Organizes information and ideas from multiple sources.	

What I Think of My Nonfiction Knowledge

I'm good at _____

because _____

I'm improving at _____

because _____

I have trouble with _____

because _____

What I Think of My Project, Report, or Presentation

The best part of my _____

was _____

because _____

I wish I had _____

because _____

Resources

Bamford, R. and Kristo, J. (2000) *Checking Out Nonfiction K–8: Good Choices for Best Learning.* Christopher-Gordon Publishers, Inc.

Bean, T. and Bishop, A. (1992) "Polar Opposites: A Strategy for Guiding Students' Critical Reading and Discussion." in Dishner, E., Bean, T. and Readence, J. (1986) *Reading in the Content Areas: Improving Classroom Instruction.* (3rd ed., pp. 247–254) Kendall/Hunt.

Beck, I. L., McKeown, M. G., Hamilton, R. L., and Kucan, L. (1997) *Questioning the Author: An Approach for Enhancing Student Engagement with Text.* International Reading Association.

Blachowicz, C. and Fisher, P. (1996) *Teaching Vocabulary in All Classrooms.* Prentice-Hall.

Blachowicz, C. and Ogle, D. (2001) *Reading Comprehension: Strategies for Independent Learners.* The Guilford Press.

Bromley, K., Irwin-Devitis, L., and Modlo, M. (1999) *Fifty Graphic Organizers for Reading, Writing, and More.* Scholastic Professional Books.

Buehl, D. (2001) *Classroom Strategies for Interactive Learning.* International Reading Association.

Burns, P., Roe, B., and Ross E. (1999) *Teaching Reading in Today's Elementary Schools.* Houghton Mifflin.

Castallo, R. (1976) "Listening Guides: A First Step Toward Notetaking and Listening Skills." *Journal of Reading*, 19, 289–290.

Cunningham, J. (1982) "Generating Interactions Between Schemata and Text," in Niles, J. and Harris, L. (eds.) *New Inquiries in Reading Research and Instruction* (pp. 42–47). Thirty-first Yearbook of the National Reading Conference in Rochester, New York.

Davis, B. and Lass, B. (1996) *Elementary Reading Strategies That Work.* Allyn and Bacon.

Frayer, D., Frederick, W., and Klausmeier, H. (1969) *A Schema for Testing the Level of Concept Mastery.* Wisconsin Research and Development Center for Cognitive Learning.

Gambrell, L., Kapinus, B., and Wilson, R. (1987) "Using Mental Imagery and Summarization to Achieve Independence in Comprehension," *Journal of Reading*, 30, 638–642.

Gere, A. (ed) (1985) *Roots in the Sawdust: Writing to Learn Across the Disciplines.* National Council of Teachers of English.

Harvey, S. (1998) *Nonfiction Matters: Reading, Writing, and Research in Grades 3–8.* Stenhouse Publishers.

Harvey, S. and Goudvis, A. (2000) *Strategies that Work.* Stenhouse Publishers.

Herber, H. (1978) *Teaching Reading in the Content Areas.* Prentice-Hall.

Hoffman, J. (1992) "Critical Reading/Thinking Across the Curriculum: Using I-charts to Support Learning," *Language Arts*, 69, 121–127.

Hunkins, F. (1995) *Teaching Thinking Through Effective Questioning.* Christopher-Gordon Publishers, Inc.

Jacobson, J. and Raymer, D. (1999) *How is My First Grader Doing in School?* Simon and Schuster.

———. (1999) *How is My Second Grader Doing in School?* Simon and Schuster.

———. (1999) *How is My Third Grader Doing in School?* Simon and Schuster.

Johnson, D. and Pearson, P. D. (1984) *Teaching Reading Vocabulary.* Rinehart and Winston.

Joyce, B. and Weil, M. (1999) *Models of Teaching.* Prentice Hall.

Resources *(cont.)*

Keene, E. O., and Zimmermann, S. (1997) *Mosaic of Thought: Teaching Comprehension in a Reader's Workshop.* Heinemann.

King, A. (1991) "Effects of Training in Strategic Questioning on Children's Problem-solving Performance." *Journal of Educational Psychology*, 83, 307–317.

Lyons, B. (1981) "The PQP Method of Responding to Writing." *English Journal*, 70, 42–43.

Manzo, A. (1969) "The ReQuest Procedure." *Journal of Reading*, 13, 123–126.

Manzo, A. and Casale, V. (1985) "Listen-read-discuss: A Content Reading Heuristic." *Journal of Reading*, 28, 732–734.

Manzo, A. and Manzo, U. (1997) *Content Area Literacy: Interactive Teaching for Interactive Learning.* Merrill.

Moore, D. W. and Moore, S. A. (1986) *Possible Sentences* in Dishner, E., Bean, T. and Readence, J. (1986) *Reading in the Content Areas: Improving Classroom Instruction.* Kendall/Hunt.

Moore, D. W., Moore, S. A., Cunningham, P. M., and Cunningham, J. W. (1998) *Developing Readers and Writers in the Content Areas K–12.* Longman.

Ogle, D. (1986) "K-W-L: A Teaching Model that Develops Active Reading of Expository Text." *The Reading Teacher*, 39, 564–570.

Parker, W. (2001) *Social Studies in Elementary Education.* Prentice-Hall.

Raphael, T. E. (1984) "Question-answering Strategies for Children." *The Reading Teacher*, 36, 186–190.

Readence, J., Bean, T., and Baldwin, R. (2000) *Content Area Literacy: An Integrated Approach.* Kendall/Hunt.

Readence, J., Moore, D., and Rickelman, R. (2000) *Prereading Activities for Content Area Reading and Learning.* International Reading Association.

Rose, L. (1991) *Picture This for Beginning Readers: Teaching Reading Through Visualization.* Zephyr Press.

Santa, C. (1988) *Content Reading Including Study Systems.* Kendall/Hunt.

Schmidt, B. and Buckley, M. (1991) Plot relationships chart. In Johns, J. and Lenski, S.D., *Improving Reading: A Handbook of Strategies.* Kendall/Hunt Publishing Company, 1997.

Searfoss, L., and Readence, J. (2000) *Helping Children Learn to Read: Creating a Classroom Literacy Environment.* Allyn and Bacon.

Stauffer, R. G. (1969) *Directing Reading Maturity as a Cognitive Process.* Harper and Row.

Tierney, R., Readence, J., and Dishner, E. (1990) *Reading Strategies and Practices: A Compendium.* Allyn and Bacon.

Vaughn, J. and Estes, T. (1986) *Reading and Reasoning Beyond the Primary Grades.* Allyn and Bacon.

Wood, K., Lapp, D., and Flood, J. (1992) *Guiding Readers through Text: A Review of Study Guides.* International Reading Association.

Zarnowski, M. (1998) "Coming Out From Under the Spell of Stories: Critiquing Historical Narratives," *New Advocate*, 11, 345–356.